WILLIAM F. BUCKLEY JR.

THE MAKER OF A MOVEMENT

WILLIAM F. BUCKLEY JR.

The Maker of a Movement

Lee Edwards

Wilmington, Delaware

Edwards, Lee.
    William F. Buckley Jr. : the maker of a movement / Lee Edwards.
    p. cm.
    Includes index.
    ISBN 1-935191-73-X

    1. Buckley, William F. (William Frank), 1925–2008. 2. Journal-
ists—United States—Biography. 3. Conservatives—United States—Biography. 4. Intellectuals—United States—Biography. 5. Conservatism—United
States—History—20th century. I. Title.

PN4874.B796E38 2010
070.92—dc22
   [B]   2009052661

ISI Books
Intercollegiate Studies Institute
3901 Centerville Road
Wilmington, DE 19807
www.isibooks.org

Manufactured in the United States of America

To Patricia Buckley Bozell

CONTENTS

PREFACE

They came from Washington, D.C., New York City, and Los Angeles, as well as places far from the centers of power. They were worldly diplomats and influential commentators, powerful politicians and popular actors, public intellectuals and legendary entrepreneurs, bestselling writers and quiet scholars. They were conservatives, libertarians, and liberals; believers and atheists; young and old; high society and Middle American; white, black, and beige—a panorama of twenty-first-century America. They came from Harvard and Yale, Hillsdale and Grove City, Notre Dame and the University of Chicago. They filled New York's St. Patrick's Cathedral that early April morning as they raised their voices in praise of an extraordinary man, William F. Buckley Jr., who had died as he had lived, at his desk, writing.

George Weigel, the author of an illuminating biography of Pope John Paul II, said that Bill Buckley was one of the most publicly influential American Catholics of the twentieth century. His ideas, wrote Weigel, "changed the way Americans think" and "reshaped our politics and our public policy."[1]

In his St. Patrick's homily, principal celebrant Rev. George W. Rutler explained that Bill Buckley's first formative academy had been his father's dinner table, where he was taught that the most important things in life are "God, truth, and beauty." Buckley adamantly opposed Communism all his life not just because it was a tyranny but also because it was a heresy. His categories, Father Rutler said, were not "Right and Left but right and wrong."[2]

Nicholas Lemann, a discerning liberal and dean of the Columbia University School of Journalism, said that during the Reagan administration "the 5,000 middle-level officials, journalists and policy intellectuals that it takes to run a government" were "deeply influenced by Buckley's example." Some of them had been personally groomed by Buckley, and "most of the rest saw him as a role model."[3]

They had been shaped by the mighty stream of words that flowed from Bill Buckley's Royal typewriter and then PC—a Mississippi River of words. Christopher Buckley, Bill and Pat Buckley's only child, recounted at the memorial mass how he had gone to the Sterling Library at Yale University to inspect his father's papers. They totaled 248.8 linear feet, higher than the spire of St. Patrick's. That did not include the 6,000 newspaper columns, 1,504 *Firing Line* television programs, and some fifty-five works of fiction and nonfiction.

Christopher leavened his remarks with a wry humor that would have pleased his father and that delighted the congregation of more than two thousand. He revealed that he and the elder Buckley had discussed his funeral service. "If I'm still famous," his father said, "try to convince the cardinal to do the service at St. Patrick's. If I'm not, just tuck me away in Stamford." Christopher acknowledged the many editorial cartoons about his father's death, including the one showing Bill Buckley at the pearly gates and St. Peter groaning, "I'm going to need a bigger dictionary." He recalled his father's appearance on ABC's *Nightline* the day he retired from his long-running television program, *Firing Line*. At the end of the interview Ted Koppel said, "Bill, we have one minute left. Would you care to sum up your thirty-three years in television?" To which Buckley replied, "No."[4]

Searching for an epitaph, Christopher recalled that his father once gave an interview to *Playboy* magazine. Asked why he had agreed to appear in so unconservative a publication, the elder Buckley replied, "In order to communicate with my sixteen-year-old son." At the interview's end he was asked what he would like for an epitaph, and he replied, "'I know that my Redeemer liveth.'" Only "Pup," Christopher said, "could manage to work the Book of Job into a Hugh Hefner publication."[5]

He ended by quoting from Robert Louis Stevenson's "Requiem," one of Bill Buckley's favorite poems:

Under the wide and starry sky,
Dig the grave and let me lie.
Glad did I live and gladly die,
And I lay me down with a will.
This be the verse you 'grave for me:

Here he lies where he long'd to be;
Home is the sailor, home from the sea,
And the hunter home from the hill.[6]

In the defiant mission statement in the first issue of *National Review,* Buckley famously wrote that his magazine would "stand athwart history, yelling Stop." But, said Michael Barone, editor of the definitive *Almanac of American Politics,* "Buckley and *National Review* did more than yell 'Stop!' at history; they turned it around, first of all by establishing a coherent and respectable conservatism." Ideas and words have power, Barone said, "and no one has shown more *joie de vivre* in deploying the power of ideas and words than William F. Buckley Jr."[7]

In his St. Patrick's eulogy, Henry Kissinger, the former secretary of state and an old friend, reminded the audience that Bill Buckley was not a utopian but a Burkean. "I believe neither in permanent victories nor in permanent defeats," Buckley would say, but he did believe in permanent values—and striving to preserve them.

"We must do what we can," Buckley once wrote Kissinger, "to bring hammer blows against the bell jar that protects the dreamers from reality." And then came this typically sinuous sentence: "The ideal scenario is that pounding from without we can effect resonances, which will one day crack through to the latent impulses of those who dream within bringing to life a circuit which will spare the republic."[8]

Shifting from the philosophical to the personal, Kissinger revealed how much Buckley's friendship had meant to him—as it had to so many. When things were really

difficult, Kissinger said—"and I mean really difficult"—
he did not have to look around to know that Bill Buckley
would "always be there beside me." With tears in his eyes,
the veteran diplomat recalled "Bill's special serenity" in
his final years. Let us all give thanks, he said, to "a benign
Providence that enabled us to walk part of our way with
this noble, gentle, and valiant man who was truly touched
by the grace of God."[9]

In the weeks following his death on February 27, 2008,
the encomiums poured forth.

"He is irreplaceable," remarked radio talkmeister Rush
Limbaugh, who described Bill Buckley as his "greatest
inspiration" from the age of twelve, when he read his first
Buckley column in the local St. Louis newspaper. Limbaugh recalled that when he was invited to an editorial
dinner at Buckley's Park Avenue home, he had his driver
go around the block a couple of times "while I built up the
courage to actually enter the place."[10]

"Before Buckley," wrote William Kristol, editor of the
neoconservative *Weekly Standard,* "there was no American
conservative movement. There were interesting (if mostly
little-known) conservative thinkers. Plenty of Americans
had conservative inclinations and sentiments. But Buckley
created conservatism as a political and intellectual movement."[11]

"He united the fragments of American conservatism,"
wrote Michael Kinsley, founder of the liberal website *Slate,*
"and paved the way for Goldwater and then Reagan."[12]

"Without Bill—if he had decided to become an
academic or a businessman or something else," said Hugh
Kenner, a biographer of Ezra Pound and a frequent con-

tributor to *National Review,* "without him, there probably would be no respectable conservative movement in this country."[13]

"Facing him," wrote Christopher Hitchens, the arch-liberal writer and militant atheist who had often appeared on *Firing Line,*

> one confronted somebody who had striven to take the "cold" out of the phrase "Cold War"; who had backed Joseph McCarthy, praised General Franco, opposed the Civil Rights Act, advocated rather than merely supported the intervention in Vietnam, and seemed meanwhile to embody a character hovering somewhere between Skull-and-Bones and his former CIA boss Howard Hunt. On the other hand, this was the same man who had picked an open fight with the John Birch Society, taken on the fringe anti-Semites and weirdo isolationists of the old Right, and helped to condition the Republican comeback of 1980. Was he really, as he once claimed, yelling "stop" at the locomotive of history, or was he a closet "progressive"?[4]

It is a provocative suggestion, but the late Tim Russert, then the moderator of NBC's *Meet the Press,* rightly emphasized that Bill Buckley was "a conservative and proud of it." He understood the rhythms of history, said Russert: "that there was a race worth running in 1964 with Barry Goldwater that would probably be unsuccessful but it would lay the groundwork for a successive takeover of the Republican Party, and the White House, to wit Ronald Reagan—and he was right."[15]

Not everyone was so complimentary, even within the conservative movement.

Christopher Westley, a professor of economics and contributor to the libertarian website LewRockwell.com, wrote disapprovingly that Buckley urged conservatives to embrace a large centralized government as "a necessary strategy to defeat the Soviets." Lew Rockwell himself described Buckley as the "enforcer of welfare-state discipline on the right," an "enabler of neoconservatism," and a "thoroughly bad ideological influence in general."[16]

The prominent paleoconservative academic Paul Gottfried quoted anti-immigration advocates Peter Brimelow and Larry Auster, who argued that Buckley had become "the captive of a leftward-moving American culture." Gottfried insisted that Buckley "had handed over American conservatism to neoconservative adventurers from the Left," making neoconservatism "the only permissible form of thinking on the right."[17]

A more favorable reading was offered by President Ronald Reagan at *National Review*'s thirtieth anniversary in 1985, when he said that the magazine and its indefatigable editor "didn't just part the Red Sea—you rolled it back, dried it up and left exposed, for all the world to see, the naked desert that is statism."

And then, as if that were not enough, the president said, "You gave the world something different, something in its weariness it desperately needed, the sound of laughter and the sight of the rich, green uplands of freedom."[18]

What shaped this polymathic, polysyllabic man, who almost single-handedly created an intellectual and political movement, uniting the several fragments of American conservatism and paving the way for Ronald Reagan, the most influential political leader in America in the second half of the twentieth century? To begin with, there were his closely knit, unshakably conservative family and his unwavering Roman Catholic faith.

CHAPTER 1

GROWING UP CONSERVATIVE

W illiam Frank Buckley Jr. was born in New York City on November 24, 1925, the sixth of the ten children of William F. Buckley Sr., a strong-willed Texan and Irish Catholic, and Aloise Steiner Buckley, the devoutly Catholic daughter of a successful New Orleans business executive. After graduating from the University of Texas, the senior Buckley made and lost a fortune in the oil fields of Mexico and then regained it in Venezuela.

In search of financing for his business ventures, he moved his large family (and two Mexican nurses) to Paris and then to London in the late 1920s and early 1930s. All of which explains, at least in part, Bill Buckley's unique accent. Until he was three, Billy Buckley was monolingual—in Spanish. His first formal schooling was in French. At five, he was enrolled in a Catholic boarding school in England. In 1933, when he was seven, the Buckley family finally settled down in Sharon, Connecticut, where Will

17

Buckley "went full-bore on implementing his pedagogical ideas."[1]

"There was nothing complicated about Father's theory of child-rearing," wrote Aloise Buckley Heath, the oldest daughter. "He brought up his sons and daughters to be absolutely perfect."[2] The son who came closest to perfection was Billy Buckley, who strove from the earliest age to please his father.

Disdaining public education for his children, Will Buckley set up his own school at Great Elm—the family home—employing a small army of private tutors. There was professional instruction in apologetics, art, calligraphy, harmony, painting, piano, speech, and typing. There were tutors in French, Latin, Spanish, and English. There were two full-time teachers, tests, grades, class hours, and requirements for graduation. Several neighborhood children also attended the Buckley "school."

What education did not occur in the classroom, writes Buckley biographer John B. Judis, took place at the dining table. The father made the children defend their intellectual and political positions. Will Buckley's dinner-table examinations "encouraged a certain kind of performing intelligence among his children." They succeeded or failed not simply by saying the right thing but by "saying it well—with wit and with style."[3] From a very early age, Billy Buckley did both. At six, according to his father, he wrote the king of England demanding that Britain pay her World War I debt.

The summers were near heaven for Billy and his siblings. They rode horses, swam in the pool, played golf or tennis, and sailed. This idyll was interrupted for forty-five minutes of piano practice every day except for the Fourth of July, Thanksgiving, Christmas—and one's birthday. There were five pianos and an organ in the house. "It was never absolutely clear," Bill Buckley later wrote, "whether the sound was worse when all the pianos were being exercised jointly or when only one of them was being played."[4]

In the mid-1930s, according to biographers Linda Bridges and John R. Coyne Jr., Will Buckley started taking his family to Camden, South Carolina, for part of the winter. He bought a house far out of town—so far that it was named Kamschatka, after the distant Siberian peninsula. "It was in Camden that the young Buckleys became acquainted with the Southern part of their heritage."[5] Most of that came from Aloise Buckley, who considered herself a "Daughter of the Confederacy." Will Buckley was a Texan, not a southerner. His grandfather had emigrated from Ireland to Canada in the 1840s and then moved his family to San Diego, Texas, a small town only a hundred miles north of the Mexican border.

The dominant personality of the family was "Father"—Will Buckley, who loved America, trusted the free market, and hated Communism with equal passion. He detested Franklin D. Roosevelt's New Deal. He did not try to mold his children into exact copies of himself, but saw to it that they were prepared, intellectually and morally, to make a difference in whatever profession they chose.

"He worshiped three earthly things," Bill Buckley later wrote, "learning, beauty, and his family." He was "the most admirable man I ever knew."[6] There was a special relationship between the father and his precocious son. Bill became "the apple of his father's eye," Jane Buckley Smith remarked. "Father loved us all," Reid Buckley said, "he respected us for our various talents, but Bill combined the intellectual brilliance with the moral control."[7]

The Buckleys were ardently Roman Catholic. While attending St. John's Beaumont, a Catholic school in England run by Jesuits, young Bill went to mass every day, praying for the health of his mother, who was in the midst of a difficult pregnancy. He achieved a special reverence for "Our Lady" (Mary, the mother of God), who "became in my mind an indispensable character in the heavenly cloister." He prayed the rosary daily for the rest of his life. It was at this time—he was thirteen—that Buckley developed what he called "a deep and permanent involvement in Catholic Christianity," a statement critical to understanding his unfailing charity as an adult—except in the case of Gore Vidal and Lowell Weicker.[8] When he was sixteen, he wrote his mother that probably the "greatest contribution you have given me is your faith. I can now rely on God in almost any matter." Years later, in his one and only book about his faith, he wrote, "I was baptized a Catholic and reared as one by devoted parents whose emotional and intellectual energies never cloyed. My faith has not wavered."[9]

At the same time, he did not hesitate to speak his mind to anyone. Within two days of his arrival at St. John's, he called at the office of the school president, a distinguished scholar, and told him there were several things about the school he did not like. The president was so shocked by the young American's boldness that he was "too paralyzed to speak," affording Bill the opportunity to explain the deficiencies of the venerable school.[10]

IN THE ARMY AND AT YALE

At fourteen, he followed his brothers to the Millbrook School, a small Protestant preparatory school in nearby New York where he boarded during the week. There Bill honed his writing and debating skills—often with the faculty. He once appeared uninvited at a faculty meeting to report that one of his teachers had deprived him of the right to express his political views in class. He proceeded to expound to the stunned faculty "on the virtues of isolationism, the dignity of the Catholic Church, and the political ignorance of the school staff."[11]

In his last year at Millbrook, he began reading—at his father's urging—the works of Albert Jay Nock, a radical libertarian who was a frequent luncheon guest at Great Elm. Born in 1870 in Scranton, Pennsylvania, author-editor Nock was a fiercely independent intellectual and severe critic of the state and of unbridled materialism. Ordained in the Episcopal Church in 1897, he served as pastor at several churches before leaving the clergy to take up a career in journalism. He was editor of *American Magazine* and then the *Nation* before becoming, in 1920, coeditor of the original *Freeman,* a magazine of politics and economics. When the *Freeman* stopped publishing for financial reasons, Nock became a freelance writer, writing pieces for a host of prominent publications and authoring several books. He penned biographies of his favorite thinkers, including Thomas Jefferson and Henry George, the leader of the "Single Tax" movement in the nineteenth century. Nock himself opposed progressive taxation.

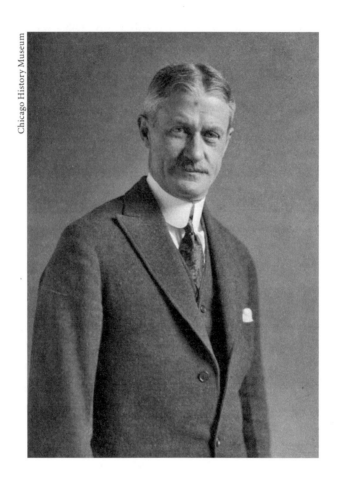

ALBERT JAY NOCK
Rejecting the welfare state

Nock's last and best-known book, *Memoirs of a Super-fluous Man,* was published in 1943, the year Buckley completed high school. In the years to come, Buckley would frequently quote from Nock's *Memoirs.* In the book, Nock invents what he calls "Epstein's Law" as an explanation of human activity: "Man tends always to satisfy his needs with the least possible exertion." As a result, Nock holds out little hope for any effective political reform. Yet he expresses an almost mystical belief in a "Remnant" of elite writers and thinkers who will one day build a new and free society on the ruins of the modern welfare state (initiated by his least favorite president, Franklin Roosevelt). *Memoirs* resonates with the conviction that, like the ancient Hebrew prophet, modern-day Isaiahs will emerge to proclaim the truth about man, the state, and liberty.[12]

A number of leading figures of the postwar Right admired Nock, including Russell Kirk, Robert Nisbet, and Frank Chodorov. They were drawn by his cutting wit— he once wrote that dogs were "natural-born New Dealers," content with whatever their masters gave them— and responded to his gospel of individual freedom.[13] Bill Buckley also admired these traits, as well Nock's passionate antistatism, his radical rhetoric, and his willingness to stick by his ideas regardless of whether they were out of step with the times. Buckley later admitted to publisher Henry Regnery that on several occasions he had made "a mental resolution" to do a book on Nock—"he has always fascinated me."[14]

Albert Jay Nock—the ultimate individualist—was the first of four conservative writers who would have a profound influence on Bill Buckley. Notably, the man who became synonymous with the term *conservative* subtitled one collection of his articles and essays *Reflections of a Libertarian Journalist.*

When Buckley graduated from Millbrook in 1943 at the head of his class, he was only seventeen, and not eligible for the draft. Not wanting to start at Yale and then leave in the middle of the school year, he spent a few months at the University of Mexico improving his Spanish before he was inducted into the army in July 1944.

Will Buckley had adamantly opposed America's entry into World War II, and his children shared his isolationist, America First views. But with Pearl Harbor, the patriotism of the Buckleys came to the fore, with John serving in the army in North Africa and France, and Jim in the navy in the Pacific.

Bill Buckley described his military service as "brief and bloodless," but it was also a rite of passage for the outspoken young conservative.[15] He did his basic training at Camp Wheeler, outside Macon, Georgia, and then in January 1945, at the age of nineteen, he entered the OCS (officers' candidate school) at Fort Benning, Georgia. Although the physical regimen was very demanding, the brash young candidate found it more difficult to be properly deferential to his superiors—and to keep his political opinions to himself. "He was very vocal about his feelings about the Democrats in general and Roosevelt in particular," recalled a friend.[16] His outspokenness did not sit well with his commanders, trained as they were to keep politics and the military separate.

After graduating from OCS—following an extended

debate by Buckley's commanding officers, who at last decided to pass him—he spent the next months as an infantry training officer at Fort Gordon, Georgia. While there he was given a singular and ironic responsibility: he was assigned to the army honor guard that stood by when the body of President Franklin D. Roosevelt was carried to the train that would take him back to Washington, D.C. With the completion of his training, Buckley was sent to Fort Sam Houston in San Antonio because of his Spanish proficiency to participate in counterintelligence activities, but he arrived the day the Japanese surrendered.

Although still not sufficiently deferential to his superiors—at least in their opinion—Bill Buckley did learn how to get along better with the men around him. In a mature letter of self-examination, he wrote to his father:

> I don't know whether you were aware of this while I was in Millbrook, but I was not very popular with boys. . . . I determined that the principal reasons for this revolved around my extreme dogmatism—particularly in matters concerning politics and the Catholic Church. I could not understand another point of view. . . .
>
> When I went into the Army, I learned the importance of tolerance, and the importance of a sense of proportion about all matters—even in regard to religion, morality etc. . . . I learned . . . that regardless of the individual's dogmas, the most important thing as far as I was concerned was the personality: would his friendship broaden your horizon or provide you with intellectual entertainment? I found that there were

actually very few prerequisites to the good friend: he
had to have a good sense of humor, a pleasant personality and a certain number of common interests.[17]

Bill Buckley had learned, as biographer John Judis writes,
to distinguish "the rules of personal friendship from those
of political combat."[18] It was a critical lesson he would
apply at Yale University and afterward.

At Yale, Buckley majored in economics, established
himself as one of the best debaters in the university's history, and was tapped by Skull and Bones, the prestigious
secret society for seniors, making him one of the biggest
men on campus. But his overriding ambition was to be
chairman of the *Yale Daily News.* "I have never run across
anything I wanted so much in all my life," he wrote his
father, "as the chairmanship of the *News.*"[19] He would
exhibit the same single-mindedness six years later when
he determined that what America needed more than anything else was a conservative journal of opinion.

Following his unanimous election, Buckley began his
year as chairman (editor-in-chief) of the newspaper on
February 1, 1949. Pre-Buckley, the *Yale Daily News* had
resembled most college papers, reporting the results of fra-
ternity elections, the latest administration press releases,
and the ups and downs of the football, basketball, and
other athletic teams. But now the *News* sent reporters to
New York and Washington to cover national stories while
Chairman Bill editorialized about Yale's educational flaws,
the dangers of Communism, the virtues of capitalism, and
the many mistakes of President Harry Truman. "There is
no indication," Buckley wrote, "that the majority of his

backers have elevated Mr. Truman to the White House to lead the United States to socialism."[20] Elsewhere he encouraged the Young Republicans, who were holding a two-day convention nearby, to reassert "the principles of freedom of enterprise [and] anti–New Dealism."[21]

Buckley editorialized often about the Soviet threat. He once asked, "Will Russia have too long to wait before she spurns [he surely meant 'thumbs'] her nose at conference and diplomacy and invades Finland and Yugoslovia and maybe even Western Germany and France?"[22] If the language seems overheated, note that in the preceding year there had been a Communist coup in Czechoslovakia, Moscow had blockaded West Berlin, the Communist Party of France had become that nation's largest political party, and Whittaker Chambers had named Alger Hiss as a Communist spy.

In another editorial, Buckley wondered why anybody would be shocked that spokesmen for the Communist Party of the United States had declared that in the event of war with Russia, American Communists would side with the Soviet Union. "We must here assert a well-known fact," he wrote. "[T]he Communist Party of the United States is an agent of Soviet Russia."[23] And after defending pre–World War II isolationism as a "sane" policy, he noted that the "world division into two ideological camps" made such isolationism in 1949 "impossible."[24]

When a reader challenged an editorial's argument that Yale University had the right, as a private institution, to exclude any and all minorities, Buckley did not back down, anticipating conservative arguments of the 1960s about civil rights legislation. We believe, he wrote, that "discrimination of sorts [is] indispensable to the free society. . . . Human beings are equal only in the eyes of God."[25]

In view of what was to come, it is significant that Bill Buckley's collegiate editorials reflected the ideas of what would become the three major strains of American conservatism in the 1950s and 1960s—traditionalism, libertarianism, and anti-Communism.

He wrote pointed commentaries about "the godless materialism" whose advance threatened civilization, about liberal hypocrites who protested the appearance of musicians who had performed in Nazi Germany but overlooked the appearances of pro-Soviet musicians like Dmitri Shostakovich, and about the views of popular Yale sociologist Raymond Kennedy, who was fond of saying that religion was a "matter of ghosts, spirits, and emotions."[26]

Anticipating a major theme of his first book, *God and Man at Yale,* Buckley wrote in the *News* that while Professor Kennedy was entitled to his own beliefs, he was not entitled to "undermin[e] religion through bawdy and slapstick humor, through circumspect allusions and emotive innuendos," particularly among freshmen and sophomores.[27] Buckley was quickly caught up in contention—in the 1940s, biographer Judis points out, students were expected to defer to their professors, not criticize them publicly. Among the irate letters to the editor was one from Professor Kennedy, who warned the twenty-three-year-old Buckley that his views would get him into trouble.[28]

Buckley shrugged off the warning from a liberal professor for whom he had little regard, but he was disturbed by the open discontent of several *Daily News* editors who called a meeting to discuss whether the chairman should submit his editorials to the whole board for approval. At the meeting, Buckley seized the offensive and called for a vote of confidence, discombobulating his colleagues, who decided not to force a vote. In a spirit of compromise, Buckley agreed to state that the editorials represented his personal views and to post for comment future editorials that might be considered controversial.[29] He prevailed and learned a key lesson: editorial control of a newspaper, or a magazine, must rest with one person, not a board.

At the end of his term as *News* chairman, Buckley wrote a series of editorials titled "What to Do?" in which he called on Yale and other universities to defend free enterprise against the challenge of socialism—another theme of *God and Man at Yale*. He wrote:

> The battle to retain free enterprise as the fundamental economic philosophy for America is being lost, and there are those of us who mind. The battle is even being lost at Yale. . . . We are losing the battle for a variety of reasons. Perhaps the most influential is the spirit of restlessness, of iconoclasm, of pragmatism that is intellectually au courant and that is warmly embraced by so many evangelistic young intellectuals who find . . . their most enthusiastic disciples in the cloistered halls of a university, where everything goes in the name of the search for truth and freedom of inquiry.[30]

For Bill Buckley, the idea of "everything goes" was absurd and to be dismissed out of hand along with pragmatism and its sibling relativism, which were at the root of the restlessness that afflicted so many young intellectuals. The answer, philosophically, was a combination of conservatism, with its emphasis on order and custom, and libertarianism, with its belief in individual freedom. Buckley called on Yale and other colleges to establish "Adam Smith chairs of Political and Economic Philosophy" in which the adherents of free enterprise could present the arguments for the system that had made America the world's most prosperous and freest nation.

In an editorial coda, Buckley pointed out that his views had been characterized as "reactionary, archaic, malicious and fascist" because, he said, he had "sallied against the stereotype liberalism which, paradoxically enough, has prescribed rigid limits to tolerable opinion in mid-twentieth-century America." But then, in a quick shift in tone, he admitted that "some of what we got we deserved" because of "the compelling urge to jolt, to ridicule, to pound square on the nose." "We deeply bemoan our inability," he sighed, "to allure without antagonizing, to seduce without violating. Especially because we believe in what we preached and would have liked very much for our vision to have been contagious."

Eschewing bathos—"it does not become us"—he concluded his chairman days with an impudent flourish: "Suffice to say that we enjoyed it all and that we hope for a Republican victory in November."[31]

For all the protests Chairman Bill sparked, he did win admirers. Commented longtime professor Paul Weiss, "There was never a time during the years I was at Yale when the paper was read so eagerly."[32] Dean William C. DeVane agreed, congratulating Buckley for "making the

News the most lively college newspaper in the country, past or present."[33]

BMOC

Buckley found other fields to conquer in college. With his roommate and future brother-in-law, L. Brent Bozell Jr., he formed one of the best debate teams in Yale history, according to debate coach Rollin Osterweis. The teammates were alike in political philosophy but dissimilar in personality and style. The rangy, red-haired Bozell offered eloquent prepared statements while Buckley engaged in "the cut-and-thrust that *Firing Line* viewers would come to know so well."[34] "They were extremely effective and dedicated," commented Alan Finberg, president of the Political Union, "and [it] struck some of us as rather unusual that people of their relatively young years could be so fiercely ideological. Many of us wished that we could be as certain about anything as they were about everything."[35]

A memorable debate occurred in the fall of 1949 when Oxford University sent over to the colonies a topflight team of Robin Day, a future celebrated journalist, and Anthony Wedgwood-Benn, who would become a leading Labour member of Parliament. Day and Wedgwood-Benn easily swept the American field until they arrived at Yale and encountered Buckley and Bozell. To the amazement of the visiting Brits, the Yale men followed an English style of debate, relying more on wit and eloquence than the usual recitation of facts and figures common to American debaters. Taking the negative side of the topic, "Resolved: the

Americans should nationalize all their non-agricultural industries," Buckley and Bozell routed the Oxford team.[36] With his debating as with his writing, Bill Buckley was perfecting his ability to convince and at the same time entertain an audience.

Buckley also found time for classes. He encountered a professor, political scientist Willmoore Kendall, who would join Albert Jay Nock as an early critical influence on his political thinking.

Kendall was born in Konowa, Oklahoma, in 1909, the son of a blind Methodist minister. He was a child prodigy who read at the age of two, and graduated from high school at thirteen and the University of Oklahoma at eighteen. He became a Rhodes scholar in 1932, spending the next four years at Oxford and in Europe, where he became sympathetic to Trotskyism. But a stint as a reporter in Madrid during the Spanish Civil War—and his witness of the Communists' deliberate murder of anyone, including newsboys, who opposed them—turned him against Communism. As historian George Nash writes, "Militant, uncompromising hostility to Communism became one of the dominant features of his thought."[37]

Entering the University of Illinois, Kendall received his Ph.D. in political science. His dissertation established him as one of the most original thinkers of political thought in America. He challenged the conventional view that John Locke was the champion of "inalienable" natural rights, arguing rather that Locke was a "majority rule" democrat. In the last analysis, he said, Locke "would entrust to the majority the power of defining individual rights," a position Kendall adopted.[38]

WILLMOORE KENDALL
Rejecting laissez-faire politics

At Yale, where he began teaching in 1947, Kendall also roundly criticized the idea of the "open society" and the notion that all questions are open questions. To the contrary, he argued, all polities, including democracies, have an orthodoxy they have a right to defend against anyone who would fundamentally change it. As Nash puts it, "The nightmare of Spain . . . taught him the horror of a society without consensus . . . a society where all people were free to talk—and talked themselves into war."[39] In the late 1940s, Kendall supported legislation outlawing the Communist Party, whose goals violated the public orthodoxy necessary for America's survival.

In later years, says Georgetown University's George Carey, Kendall "refined his views considerably in light of the American political system."[40] According to Carey, Kendall argued that the founding fathers placed a premium on achieving consensus "rather than simply counting heads" and intended Congress to express the popular will through such consensus. However, liberals had succeeded in establishing the president as "the most authentic representative of the people's values and aspirations."[41] As a result, there were "two majorities" in America—the congressional majority based on the values and interests of the thousands of communities across the country, and the presidential majority, which spoke for the people as a mass. Kendall asserted that Congress as an institution was inherently more conservative than the presidency.[42]

Enrolling in Kendall's political science seminar, Buckley became a political disciple and personal friend of the "wild Yale don." Kendall taught the young conservative to read political theory with the close attention to the text that the political philosopher Leo Strauss advocated. "Bill always had so much intellectual energy," recalled Charles Lichenstein, a graduate student of Kendall, "that he threatened to run off in too many directions simultaneously. Willmoore helped him enormously to focus that energy, target that energy, to encourage a higher degree of discipline."[43]

Kendall also exerted an enormous influence on Buckley's political thought. In fact, Buckley later said, "I attribute whatever political and philosophical insights I have to his tutelage and his friendship."[44]

Buckley was genuinely struck by Kendall's Nock-like metaphor—constantly used in class—that the conservative forces were strung out in isolated outposts over a wide front. As Carey summarizes Kendall's "battlefield metaphor," liberals could "easily overrun" those outposts "one at a time because they possessed a general staff to concentrate and coordinate their forces for attack. Only when these conservative outposts united in the recognition of their common enemy would conservatism prevail."[45] Buckley would promote and adhere to a strategy of unity as editor of *National Review*. Indeed, he would become the commander that conservatism had lacked.

Kendall, with his "militant, uncompromising" hostility to Communism, also reinforced Buckley's already fervent anti-Communism. What's more, with his rejection of laissez-faire politics, he provided Buckley with a key argument for the young man's critique of what in *God and Man at Yale* would be called "laissez-faire" academic freedom.

Despite the extraordinary effect Kendall had on him, Buckley was of two minds about majority politics. He was an elitist, but also said he would rather be governed by the first two thousand names in the Boston telephone directory rather than the Harvard faculty. As we will see, and consistent with his evolving fusionism, he set aside his libertarianism and accepted a large role for the federal government because of the express need to resist Communism. At the same time, he did not hesitate to criticize the actions of whoever was in the White House, whether he was a Republican or a Democrat—from Harry Truman to George W. Bush.

While Kendall influenced Buckley, the student may have influenced his mentor—with his deeply grounded faith. In 1949 Kendall was, in Buckley's words, "rather cynical about the great truths" that directed society. But by the mid-1950s Kendall had become "one of the few fine and intensely moral figures of our time." In 1956 Kendall converted to Roman Catholicism, inspired in part, he said, by the church's centuries of tradition.[46]

Like Nock, Kendall delighted in going against the grain. "He was a conservative all right," Buckley remembered, "but invariably he gave the impression that he was being a conservative because he was surrounded by liberals; that he'd have been a revolutionist if that had been required in order to be socially disruptive."[47]

Throughout his time at Yale, Buckley never hesitated to make his own conservative political views known, relishing the controversy they created among students and faculty. Henry Wallace's third-party 1948 campaign for the presidency inspired him to take direct political action. Although Wallace had little chance of winning the election, he was pro-Soviet and anti-anti-Communist, sufficient reason for Buckley to lead a protest against Wallace's appearance in the New Haven Arena. Buckley, his sisters Patricia and Jane, and several of his friends dressed up as ultraleftists—the girls wore dark suits and no makeup, the boys dark suits, loud ties, and greased hair—and carried signs saying, "Let's Prove We Want Peace—Give Russia the Atom Bomb."

In April, Buckley and Kendall debated two Wallace supporters on radio. When Nathaniel Colley, one of the Wallaceites, threatened to sue Kendall for an intemperate remark, Buckley challenged Colley to sue him instead and wrote in the *Yale Daily News*, "The undeniable facts are: [Professor] Nathaniel S. Colley, through his support of Henry Wallace, is—be it unwittingly—furthering the ends of the Soviet Union."[48]

Colley did not take the bait, but Buckley was confirmed in his lifelong application of the French revolutionary Danton's philosophy, "De l'audace, encore de l'audace, et toujours de l'audace."[49]

Buckley's Yale years reached a climax in February 1950 when he was chosen by the faculty (who apparently had not been paying close attention to the *Yale Daily News*) to be the student speaker at Alumni Day. Rather than writing the expected "good old Yale" speech, he discussed the "policy of educational laissez-faire," or academic freedom—borrowing from Kendall's critique of laissez-faire politics. According to Buckley, it was against "academic freedom" to insist that freedom was better than tyranny, the free market better than socialism and central planning, and Christianity better than secular humanism. The problem, Buckley said, was not that all Yale professors were hard-core atheists or socialists but that the administration declined to say that one set of opinions was better than the other.[50] For Buckley, it was obvious which was better.

When he submitted a copy of his speech, he was asked by a leading alumnus to alter his "indictment of the administration" because the alumni "simply wouldn't understand it." Buckley changed a couple of sentences. When pressed to do more rewriting, he declined and offered to withdraw as speaker. Despite more appeals to soften his criticism, Buckley remained adamant. Finally, Yale president Charles Seymour personally accepted his withdrawal.[51]

But this was not the final chapter of Bill Buckley's career at Yale. As part of graduation exercises—he graduated with honors—he was elected by the Yale class council to deliver the class oration. An apprehensive administration hesitated but did not try to persuade the students to select another speaker. Although still vexed over the cancellation of his Alumni Day speech, Buckley did not single out the administration but called on the university to return to promoting Western civilization and praising America as "an oasis of freedom and prosperity."[52]

Thank God that's over, relieved administration officials undoubtedly said to themselves, not realizing they had provided William F. Buckley Jr. with the theme of his first book.

GOD AND MAN AND MARRIAGE

Through his sister Patricia, Bill Buckley met Patricia Taylor of Vancouver, Canada, who was beautiful, as sharp-witted as Bill, and even wealthier. "Pat looks like a queen, she acts like a queen, and is just the match for Billy," remarked his sister.[53] After a brief period of courting, Bill flew to Vancouver for a weekend and on the third day asked Pat if she would marry him. "She rushed upstairs to tell her mother," Buckley recalled,

> and I waited at the bottom of the huge staircase hoping to get the temper of her proud mother's reaction (her father was out of town), and soon I heard peals of laughter. I waited apprehensively for Pat to advise me what that was all about. The laughter, she revealed, was generated by her mother's taking the occasion to recall that eight times in the past, Pat had reported her betrothal.[54]

Bill and Pat—an Anglican—married in July 1950 at the Roman Catholic cathedral in Vancouver and then were blessed by the Anglican bishop at their wedding reception. They would love, honor, and challenge each other for more than five decades, until Pat Buckley's death in April 2007.

The young couple settled in Hamden, Connecticut, a New Haven suburb, where Buckley taught Spanish part-time at Yale while working on a book dealing with the themes of his never-delivered Alumni Day talk—socialism versus capitalism and secularism versus Christianity at Yale. He was helped by his friend Frank Chodorov, a disciple of the archlibertarian Albert Jay Nock, and Willmoore Kendall, who read the manuscript and made numerous suggestions. Buckley would continue the practice of submitting his latest work-in-progress to selected friends and family members for their comments for the rest of his life.

While settling into his marriage and working on his first book, Buckley was also waiting to hear about a possible new job—a post with the Central Intelligence Agency. Even before his graduation, he had talked to the CIA at the suggestion of Kendall, who offered to introduce Buckley to James Burnham, then a consultant to the agency and someone whom Kendall idolized. When Kendall talked about Burnham in class, Buckley recalled, it was as if he were "describing Wotan."[55] Buckley would come to hold almost as high an opinion of Burnham during Burnham's long tenure as *National Review*'s most important senior editor. James Burnham became the third major influence on Bill Buckley's political thinking.

Born in Chicago in 1905, Burnham graduated at the top of his class at Princeton and then—like Willmoore Kendall—entered Oxford, where he studied English literature and medieval philosophy. He joined the faculty of New York University and served as a professor of philosophy from 1929 to 1953. Drawn to politics during the Great Depression and fearful of the survival of Western civilization, he became a Trotskyite—also like Kendall. In fact, Burnham helped form the Socialist Workers Party and became a leading disciple of Leon Trotsky. Burnham broke with Trotsky when the old Bolshevik defended the Soviet Union even after Stalin's invasion of Finland and takeover of the Baltic states. But it's noteworthy that both Burnham and Kendall—and as we will see, the fourth major influence on Buckley—were former members of the Left who could provide personal testimony about (to paraphrase

JAMES BURNHAM
Apostle of realpolitik

Arthur Koestler) the necessary lies, slanders, intimidations, and liquidations of Marxism-Leninism.[56]

In 1941 Burnham published *The Managerial Revolution,* which described the emergence of a new and unelected ruling elite, the managerial class, and its profound implications for Western society. In subsequent books, Burnham argued that the Soviet Union was the most advanced managerial regime and sought global power through subversion, aggression, and intimidation—an argument that Buckley fully endorsed.

Burnham was an apostle of realpolitik both in U.S. foreign policy and in politics. His pragmatism would profoundly shape Buckley, his magazine, and ultimately the conservative movement he led. Buckley would later write to Burnham: "It is inconceivable that *NR* could have lasted as a significant journal of opinion without your self-effacing contributions to it, and to my education, and morale." He added, speaking objectively he insisted, that "your influence, as a great teacher and as a great analyst, has permanently affected the thought of those in America who will be making the substantial arguments in the days to come."[57]

Buckley traveled to Washington in June 1950 to talk to Burnham about his prospective CIA employment. There he met Howard Hunt—later known for his role in the Watergate break-in. Hunt had already served in the Office of Strategic Services (OSS), the precursor to the CIA, and written a bestselling novel, and he was about to take over the agency's operations in Mexico City. He was impressed by the young Yale graduate, who spoke fluent Spanish and had already lived in Mexico City. Burnham described

Buckley as "a committed and articulate anti-Communist looking for the optimum way of working against the Stalinists." "I needed somebody [outside the embassy]," Hunt later said, "who could make contacts and deal with the young people."[58]

Back in Connecticut, Buckley applied the finishing touches to his manuscript about Yale and began looking for a publisher outside New York. He was certain that no mainline publishing house would touch his book. Frank Chodorov wrote to Henry Regnery, a conservative Chicago publisher, urging him to consider publishing the first work of a promising young writer named William F. Buckley Jr. Regnery liked the manuscript and scheduled publication for October 1951, with a first printing of five thousand copies, an impressive number for an unknown author. When *God and Man at Yale* quickly became a bestseller, Regnery ordered a second printing and sold twelve thousand copies in November alone. The book's success can be attributed in part to Regnery's extensive advertising campaign, which was largely underwritten by Will Buckley Sr.[59] A condition of the Buckley investment was that the book would come out by the end of October, when Yale would celebrate its 250th anniversary.

The book—and Buckley himself—came under withering attack from Yale and from mainstream newspapers and journals. Some praised the work, including the onetime socialist Max Eastman, who lauded the author's "arrant intellectual courage." The *New Republic*'s Selden Rodman declared that Buckley wrote with "a clarity, a sobriety, and an intellectual honesty that would be noteworthy if it came from a college president."[60]

The critical nadir was reached by Yale trustee Frank Ashburn, who wrote in *Saturday Review*: "The book is one which has the glow and appeal of a fiery cross on a hillside at night. There will undoubtedly be robed figures who gather to it, but the hoods will not be academic. They will cover the face."[61]

What had Buckley written that so enraged his alma mater and its establishment friends? He charged that Yale's values were agnostic as to religion, "interventionist" and Keynesian as to economics, and collectivist as regards the relation of the individual to society and government. While conceding the validity of academic freedom for a professor's research, Buckley insisted that the professor did not have the right to inseminate into the minds of his students values that were counter to the values of the parents paying his salary. He urged parents, alumni, and trustees to resist this aberrant form of academic freedom.

Drawing upon his university experience, Buckley submitted that Yale had abandoned Christianity, free enterprise, and what he called "individualism." (He described himself in these early days as an "individualist" rather than a conservative.) He said that the faculty members who fostered atheism and socialism ought to be fired, because the primary goal of education is to familiarize students with an existing body of truth, of which Christianity and free enterprise are the foundations. "Individualism is dying at Yale," Buckley declared, "and without a fight."[62]

As Buckley biographer Judis puts it, *God and Man at Yale* assumed the existence of a liberal establishment of administration and faculty that ruled without a mandate over students and alumni. The young author called "upon the conservative majority to rise up and overthrow the liberal elite."[63]

In April 1951, as he was finishing *God and Man at Yale,* Buckley was told that he had been accepted by the CIA. After training in Washington, D.C., he would be assigned to Mexico City. While in Washington, he also worked at *Human Events,* the weekly newsletter edited by conservative Frank Hanighen and libertarian Frank Chodorov. It fell to Chodorov to publish Bill Buckley's first professional article that spring, "Harvard Hogs the Headlines," paying him the munificent sum of twenty-five dollars. Buckley wrote that although Harvard "gets most of the credit for nourishing the new, irresistible, mid-century liberalism—collectivism," Yale deserved just as much credit.[64] Buckley later wrote of Chodorov's tutelage: "It is quite unlikely that I should have pursued a career as a writer but for the encouragement he gave me just after I graduated from Yale."[65] Typical of Chodorov's pungent advice to the young writer: "The day you don't sit at a typewriter for three hours is a day wasted."[66]

In Mexico City, Buckley quickly developed contacts within the student movements, edited an anti-Communist book written by a former prominent Chilean Communist, and greatly impressed Howard Hunt, who had not realized in their first meetings "how well read and politically educated he was." But the operational life of an agent—the tedium of making hundreds of telephone calls and contacts with the hope that a couple would prove useful—began to pale. There was too little romance and too much routine for the restless Buckley.[67]

Eager to get on with changing the intellectual climate

of America, encouraged by the brisk sales of *God and Man at Yale,* and responsive to Pat's wishes—she was pregnant and didn't want to give birth to a child in Mexico City—Buckley informed Hunt in February 1952 that he was going to resign from the CIA and return home. He had been a secret agent for only nine months, but he used the experience to create a memorable fictional character, Blackford Oakes, the bold and brainy CIA hero of his popular novels about the Cold War.

Hunt was not surprised at Buckley's decision. "I felt Bill had a great deal of drive to excel," he recalled, "to become a figure with a capital F, and a spokesman, a man who wanted to present his ideas and his philosophy in very broad and significant forums. Obviously this wasn't possible given the limitations of the CIA."[68]

Searching for a Magazine

Will Buckley suggested that his son do graduate study at Oxford or Cambridge; Henry Regnery thought the young author could benefit by studying under the free-market economist F. A. Hayek at the University of Chicago. But Bill Buckley wanted to make a difference without delay. He entered the field in which he would play a leading role for the rest of his life—journalism. He accepted an offer from the *American Mercury* (turning down the *Freeman*) when its editor, William Bradford Huie, promised Buckley significant responsibility and freedom as associate editor. It also mattered that the *Mercury,* with 90,000 subscribers, had four times the circulation of the *Freeman.*

But within a few weeks of starting the job, Buckley fell out with the other associate editor, Martin Greenburg, when he refused to publish Buckley's critical article about liberal dominance in the realm of ideas, ironically titled "The Plight of the Liberals." Buckley quit the magazine. Declining an offer from the *Freeman,* he retired to his new home on Wallacks Point in Stamford, Connecticut, overlooking Long Island Sound, to write and to enjoy his new son, Christopher, born in September 1952. Buckley did not have to look very far to find an appropriate book topic.

Because of his militant anti-Communism, Senator Joseph McCarthy of Wisconsin had become the hero of millions of Main Street Americans and the bête noire of the liberal establishment. Both Buckley and Brent Bozell admired McCarthy for his willingness to take on the liberal elite and began writing a long article about the outspoken senator. When Henry Regnery suggested they expand it into a book, they readily agreed. The result was *McCarthy and His Enemies,* which examined the senator's record and his opponents through 1952.

Occupied with the McCarthy book and carrying a heavy speaking schedule, the twenty-six-year-old Buckley nevertheless agreed, at the invitation of Frank Chodorov, to become president of a new national student organization—the Intercollegiate Society of Individualists (later renamed the Intercollegiate Studies Institute). It was his first conscious act of building a conservative movement.

Buckley and ISI were a perfect match. ISI's articles of incorporation stated that its objective was "to promote among college students, specifically, and the public, generally, an understanding of and appreciation for the

Constitution of the United States of America, laissez-faire (free market) economics and the doctrine of individualism." But in early 1953, less than a year later, Chodorov informed Buckley in a note: "Am removing you as president. Making myself pres. Easier to raise money if a Jew is president. You can be V-P. Love, Frank." A busy Buckley was relieved to be relieved, but remained an enthusiastic supporter of ISI's activities and publications—appearing on many campuses under its sponsorship—for the rest of his life.[69]

Meanwhile, Henry Regnery commissioned Willi Schlamm, a brilliant *Time*-tested editor, to shorten the 250,000-word manuscript submitted by Buckley and Bozell and to write an introduction. While they were working together, Schlamm shared with Buckley his long-held dream of starting a weekly conservative journal of opinion. He secured Buckley's commitment to the undertaking with the understanding that the twenty-eight-year-old American wunderkind would serve as editor-in-chief and the forty-seven-year-old Austrian intellectual and former Communist as senior editor and éminence grise.[70]

The assent flowed from two factors. The first was that Buckley himself had been thinking about starting a magazine, mentioning it to Howard Hunt when he left the CIA in 1952 and to his Yale friend Evan Galbraith when he joined the *American Mercury*. He had sought the advice of Henry Regnery, who suggested that he edit a monthly magazine along with another Regnery author, Russell Kirk, but Buckley was not interested in a scholarly journal of limited circulation and influence.[71]

The second factor in Buckley's decision was the intellectual vacuum that existed in the still amorphous conservative movement. The failing *Freeman* was bought by Leonard Read of the Foundation for Economic Freedom, who turned it into an economic monthly, "staid and academic," in Buckley's words. The *American Mercury* was taken over by millionaire Russell Maguire, a rabid anti-Semite, who immediately began filling the once-influential magazine with anti-Semitic diatribes.[72]

Impressed by Buckley's ambition and resources, Schlamm argued that the youthful Buckley should be the undisputed editor of their magazine precisely because he was under thirty. "It was much easier for a 29-year-old to be editor-in-chief of a magazine with these giants than for a 39-year-old or a 49-year-old," Buckley recalled Schlamm saying, "because people are willing to do favors and be condescending toward someone who was 25 years younger than they."[73] The "giants" referred to were authors such as James Burnham, Whittaker Chambers, and Russell Kirk, whom the editors intended to recruit.

Schlamm's other recommendation was that Buckley be the journal's sole owner and stockholder so that factionalism would not wreck the new magazine as it had the *Freeman*. According to author and columnist John Chamberlain, who knew both men, Schlamm was confident he "could maintain his influence over a young man who was all of twenty-nine years old and was just feeling his way amid the complexities of a Stalin-dominated world."[74] Schlamm's shrewd plan to make Buckley the formal and legal head of the new magazine—a proposition Buckley readily accepted—would enable the publication to survive the inevitable internal disputes, including the first serious quarrel, precipitated by none other than Willi Schlamm.[75]

Buckley acknowledged Schlamm's essential role in an early *NR* memorandum to James Burnham when he said flatly, "It was Willi who dreamed of the magazine, and who persuaded me to make the effort to launch it. I am a fairly enterprising fellow, but I would not have thought of going out myself to found one." It took Schlamm's prodding and generosity, he told Burnham, as well as that "of yourself and of others, to convince me that . . . the idea of such a magazine was not grotesque; that the magazine was desprately [*sic*] needed; and, even, that the magazine might succeed."[76]

But first came *McCarthy and His Enemies.*

As the historian George Nash points out, Buckley and Bozell strove for balance in their analysis, criticizing McCarthy for being guilty of blunders and "outrageous" conduct. But for all his faults, the authors concluded, the senator was correct: there were Communists in the U.S. government, which had been incredibly negligent in failing to oust the many security risks. As for McCarthy's rhetorical excesses, they were no more objectionable than those of other partisan politicians of the day, including Harry Truman.[77]

In his 1948 election campaign, President Truman said at one rally that a vote for the Republican candidate, New York governor Thomas Dewey, was "a vote for fascism." At another event, he suggested that the Communists were hoping for a Republican victory because they believed that would mean "a weak United States."[78]

"On McCarthyism," wrote Buckley and Bozell bluntly, "hang the hopes of America for effective resistance to Communist infiltration. . . . [A]s long as McCarthyism fixes its goal with its present precision, it is a movement around which men of good will and stern morality can close ranks."[79]

Once again, Bill Buckley was plunged into controversy. *McCarthy and His Enemies* was published in March 1954, one month before the nationally televised Army-McCarthy hearings. Buckley and Bozell were inundated with invitations to speak and debate and appear on radio. They trounced two Yale law professors in a debate at the university, with Buckley receiving "a long and loud burst of applause" at the end of his remarks, as the *Yale Daily News* reported. More than a thousand people filled the auditorium of the National Republican Club in New York City to hear Buckley denounce the Republicans who were turning away from McCarthy.[80]

Buckley tapped into a new constituency for American conservatism—middle-class Catholic Democrats, who would later form an important part of the Reagan coalition. Catholic groups in Queens, New York, and the suburbs of other eastern cities asked the young author to speak. They looked to Buckley as a Catholic "who understood McCarthy."[81] Judis, a liberal, argues that Buckley's defense of McCarthy made him "a pariah" among the eastern intelligentsia, but he was a hero among anti-Communists and conservatives across the country—a reputation that would help when he launched *National Review.*

Then and always, Buckley honored the principle of standing by your friends and colleagues when they are under attack. Before and after the Senate censure of McCarthy in December 1954, the McCarthys, the Buckleys, and the Bozells remained personal friends. Bill Buckley never publicly disassociated himself from the man or the *ism,* convinced as he was of the necessity of combating Communism at home and abroad.

In a 1977 review of *Tail Gunner Joe,* a network television dramatization, Buckley scorned the anti-McCarthy bias of the program, writing, "There were some foolish things done and said by McCarthy and some of his supporters during the Fifties. But they cannot hold a candle up against the continuing excesses of McCarthy's critics."[82]

Four decades after McCarthy's death, Buckley wrote *The Redhunter: A Novel Based on the Life of Senator Joe McCarthy,* in which he rejects the liberal view that McCarthy spawned a "reign of terror" that gripped professors, writers, actors, public officials, plumbers, and ordinary citizens from one coast to another. But he does offer a candid portrait of a man who will distort the truth to make a point and blacken the reputation of an opponent without apology, and who cannot slake his thirst for bourbon, vodka, or whatever brand of booze is readily available.

In the novel, Yale professor Willmoore Sherriff (closely modeled on Willmoore Kendall) criticizes McCarthy's gutter style but nevertheless defends him because the senator understands that the function of a "vital democratic society" is to "reject unassimilable ideas" such as Communism. Biographer Sam Tanenhaus says that this defense "comes close to Buckley's own view of McCarthyism, scarcely altered since 1954."[83]

In an introduction to a 1961 edition of *McCarthy and His Enemies,* Buckley wrote, "The McCarthy business of course was deadly serious, and if it was not, there surely was no excuse either for his activities or his enemies." The "deadly" business Buckley referred to was not McCarthyism but Communism.[84]

How unyielding an anti-Communist Buckley was can be seen in his January 1952 essay in *Commonweal*. Buckley wrote that given the "thus-far invincible aggressiveness of the Soviet Union . . . we have got to accept Big Government for the duration." The chances of "ultimate victory against an indigenous bureaucracy," he said, "are far greater than they could ever be against one controlled from abroad, one that would be nourished and protected by a worldwide Communist monolith."[85] Buckley's willingness, in the face of the Soviet threat, to accept "Big Government" was roundly criticized by libertarians. But he did not flinch, believing that in the present crisis a substantial defense establishment was required to preserve liberty.

As 1954 ended, the future of the American Right seemed uncertain. "Mr. Republican" Robert Taft was dead of cancer, Joe McCarthy had been censured by his peers, the Democrats had retaken Congress after a brief Republican interregnum, President Eisenhower had morphed into a modern Republican, and Barry Goldwater was an unknown junior senator from Arizona. When Russell Kirk published his intellectual history of Anglo-American conservatism in 1953, he at first intended to title it *The Conservative Rout*. At a moment when Lionel Trilling's complaint that conservatism expressed itself only in "irritable mental gestures" seemed painfully apt, William F. Buckley Jr. began the most far-reaching adventure of his life—the creation of a conservative journal that would challenge the liberal zeitgeist and, more than any other institution, mold a national movement that would dominate American politics in the 1980s and beyond.

CHAPTER 2

GETTING IT RIGHT

Present at the creation of *National Review* were tradi-tional conservatives Russell Kirk and Richard Weaver, libertarians John Chamberlain and Frank Chodorov, and, by far the largest group, anti-Communists who were also ex-Communists: James Burnham, Frank Meyer, Willi Schlamm, Willmoore Kendall, Freda Utley, Max Eastman, and Whittaker Chambers (who did not formally become an editor until 1957). It was Bill Buckley's special genius as a fusionist that he was able to keep these philosophically dissimilar and disputatious writers on the same masthead for years to come.

Why were there so few defectors? Because of Buckley's extraordinary skill at honoring and integrating the con-flicting voices of the conservative choir. And because one and all realized, eventually, that they were part of some-thing historic—what Buckley would come to call "our movement."[1]

But first Buckley had to raise an estimated $550,000 (equal to $4.4 million in 2010) to underwrite the costs of the magazine until it had a sufficient number of subscribers and advertisers. The young editor-in-chief-to-be went calling on wealthy conservatives in the Midwest, the Deep South (textile manufacturer Roger Milliken, a Yale graduate, signed a large advertising contract on behalf of the Deering-Milliken Company), and Texas, where Buckley was judged by billionaire oilman H. L. Hunt and other Texans to be too Catholic, too eastern, and too moderate. (Not even Will Buckley's Texas background made a difference.) Hollywood was surprisingly receptive, primarily because of the award-winning screenwriter Morrie Ryskind (among his credits, the Marx Brothers' films), who introduced Buckley to John Wayne, Bing Crosby, Adolphe Menjou, Ward Bond, and other conservative film stars as well as wealthy conservative businessmen Henry Salvatori and Frank Seaver.

One of the most enthusiastic endorsements of the magazine came from candy manufacturer Robert Welch, who wrote: "Here is wishing for NATIONAL REVIEW a rapid and continuing growth in readership, influence, and effectiveness. May it become a mighty factor in saving our country from further follies of collectivism and the Communist menace behind them."[2] Welch, soon to found the John Birch Society, would come to regret his early support for the magazine.

Buckley attempted to assist the launch of his new publication by eliminating the competition. He tried to buy both *Human Events* and the *Freeman. Human Events* editor Frank Hanighen turned down Buckley's offer of $30,000, while the directors of the Foundation for Economic Education unanimously rejected Buckley, with one director explaining that "the *Freeman* cannot go out of business without doing the cause a tremendous amount of harm."[3]

By September 1955, Buckley had raised only $290,000 from the outside plus $100,000 from the magazine's first and most enthusiastic backer, his father. What should we do? Buckley asked Willi Schlamm. Go ahead and publish, asserted the veteran editor, arguing that if they succeeded in attracting twenty-five thousand readers, the subscribers would not let the magazine die.[4] Schlamm's prediction turned out to be correct.

In addition to fundraising, Buckley was busy trying to enlist the right people to edit his magazine. He had three men in mind as senior editors: James Burnham, Whittaker Chambers, and Russell Kirk. Their differing philosophies are telling. Burnham was a Trotskyite turned realpolitik conservative. Chambers was a former Soviet spy who now called himself a man of the Right. Kirk was a traditional midwestern conservative. Buckley was not interested in ideologues; he wanted men of experience and wisdom who shared his vision of a conservative counterestablishment.

The young editor was partially successful in his recruiting. Burnham, who had left the CIA and had been asked to leave *Partisan Review* for being too sympathetic to Joe McCarthy, quickly accepted Buckley's offer. He too had been thinking about a weekly magazine that dealt with the issues of the day. He was Buckley's first recruit and would become first among equals of the senior editors.

Buckley now trained his sights on Russell Kirk, a far different kind of conservative from Burnham. Born in the village of Plymouth, Michigan, in 1918, Kirk was a romantic, and a traditionalist who rejected the "assembly-line civilization" of Henry Ford. After graduating from Michigan State College in 1940, Kirk headed south to Duke University, where he earned a master's degree in history under the tutelage of two distinguished scholars in history and literature, Charles Sydnor and Jay Hubbell. His thesis was published as his first book—*Randolph of Roanoke: A Study in Conservative Thought.*

Although he believed that all the wars fought by the American people might have been averted, Kirk was drafted into the army in the summer of 1942 and rose to the rank of sergeant while serving in the Chemical Warfare Service in the United States. His duties were such that he was able to read deeply in Marcus Aurelius, Epictetus, Seneca, and Albert Jay Nock, with whom he briefly corresponded before Nock's death in 1945.

Upon being discharged, Kirk returned to Michigan State, where he taught history to students more interested in animal husbandry than the founding, opened a used bookstore, and founded the George Ade Society (named after the Indiana humorist), at whose meetings members discussed the works of Richard Weaver, author of *Ideas Have Consequences,* and Ross J. S. Hoffman, the Burke scholar.

Unwilling to remain buried academically in Michigan, and proud of his Scottish ancestry, Kirk wrote to the secretary of the University of St. Andrews, inquiring whether he might be admitted as a candidate for St. Andrews's highest arts degree, doctor of letters. He stated his intention to write a book about Edmund Burke's thought. On a monthly stipend of seventy-five dollars from St. Andrews plus the G.I. Bill, Kirk began his studies at Scotland's oldest university. In 1952 he received a doctorate in literature from St. Andrews, the first American ever to do so. He also completed a highly praised dissertation on Anglo-American thought over the past 175 years that became *The Conservative Mind*—a work that transformed public understanding of American conservatism.

In 1954, when Bill Buckley came calling, Kirk was happily ensconced in tiny isolated Mecosta, Michigan, where he could read and write all day and all night. He had no intention of removing himself to New York City, where the new magazine would be headquartered, and he was adamant about not associating with what he called "the Supreme Soviet of Libertarianism," represented by Frank Chodorov and Frank Meyer. Kirk was still incensed over Meyer's charge in the *Freeman* that he and other "new conservatives" had no grounding in "clear and distinct principle." According to Meyer, Kirk did not comprehend the principles and institutions of a free society.[5]

Undaunted, Buckley traveled to Mecosta. After a long evening of Tom Collinses and conversation about the world, the flesh, and the devil, Kirk agreed to write a regular column in the magazine about higher education in America, although he declined to serve as a senior editor. Buckley worked hard to maintain the Kirk-*NR* relationship, recognizing the author of *The Conservative Mind* as a preeminent voice of conservatism. He reassured Kirk that Chodorov and Meyer did not bear any malice toward him but attached "a great deal of importance to one aspect of the current [philosophical] controversy." Buckley tried to apply fusionist balm to the controversy, writing Kirk that "just as you reproach them for being too sectarian, I would reproach any magazine that closed its eyes to the transcendent affinities between you and Meyer and chose to be so sectarian as to run only the one or the other."[6]

Buckley next turned to Whittaker Chambers, the former Communist agent and *Time* magazine editor. Chambers had been at the center of a national controversy in 1948, when he served as chief witness in the Alger Hiss spy case, testifying that the debonair New Dealer—a former high-ranking State Department official and the secretary-general at the United Nations' founding conference—had been a Soviet operative in the 1930s. Chambers's Dostoyevskian memoir, *Witness,* published in 1952, had mesmerized Buckley. Together with Schlamm, Buckley made several visits to Chambers's Maryland farm to attempt to bring the writer and editor on board at his new magazine. Buckley and Chambers also engaged in extensive correspondence, in which Buckley sought to allay any doubts Chambers might have, even offering at one point to remove himself as editor if that was an obstacle to Chambers's participation.

In the process, Buckley and Chambers became friends, but Chambers nevertheless said no. Buckley thought the reason was that he and the magazine entertained doubts "about Richard Nixon's fitness to succeed Eisenhower," who had just suffered a heart attack and, it was rumored, would not seek a second presidential term. Chambers had never forgotten that Nixon, as a member of the House Committee on Un-American Activities, had believed Chambers's testimony and not Alger Hiss's about their espionage activities for the Soviets. Biographer Judis suggests Chambers believed that Buckley and his colleagues were too ideological, whereas he preferred the "Beaconsfield position," a more pragmatic approach to politics. "That is what conservatives must decide," Chambers wrote Buckley, "how much to give in order to survive at all; how much to give in order not to give up the basic principles."[7]

Jeffrey Hart, who served as a senior editor of *National Review* for more than thirty years and wrote a perceptive history of the magazine, regards the issue Chambers raised as central to the evolution of *National Review*—and, this writer adds, to the American conservative movement.

It can be framed, according to Hart, as the choice "between ideal right-wing Paradigm and realistic Possibility." Chambers described his politics as "dialectical." That is, he would assess a political situation as accurately as he could and then take corrective action. The result might be only a small gain, but a gain was better than nothing. Over the years, says Hart, James Burnham would come to "embody that strategy gradually prevailing over Buckley's 'ideal' impulses." The cumulative effect was to move Bill Buckley toward a Chambers-Burnham realism—and "the magazine toward greater effectiveness."[8]

Joining Albert Jay Nock, Willmoore Kendall, and James Burnham, Whittaker Chambers was the fourth seminal influence on Buckley's political thinking. When Chambers died in 1961, Buckley compared his singular "voice" to that of the famed Wagnerian soprano Kirsten Flagstad, saying it was "magnificent in tone, speaking to our time from the center of sorrow, from the center of the earth."[9]

WHITTAKER CHAMBERS
The most important American defector
from Communism

In *Witness,* Chambers tells the story of his youthful disillusion with the West, participation in espionage at high
levels of the U.S. government, and final break with Communism after Stalin's "great terror" of 1937–38. Chambers
argues that America faces a transcendent, not transitory,
crisis; that the crisis is not one of politics or economics but
of faith; and that secular liberalism, the dominant *ism* in
America, is a watered-down version of Communist ideology. The New Deal, he insists, is not liberal democratic but
"revolutionary" in its nature and intentions. In his "Fore-
word in the Form of a Letter to My Children," Chambers
writes that Communism is "the central experience of the
first half of the 20th century, and may be its final experience" unless the free world discovers a "power of faith"
that will provide two certainties: "a reason to live and a
reason to die."[10]

Along with Kendall and Burnham, Chambers—the
most important American defector from Communism—
confirmed Buckley's belief that Communism was the overriding issue, and challenge, confronting America. Chambers's linking of liberalism and Communism helped to
justify Buckley's ready condemnation of the Left in every
available forum. Burnham would make the same point in
Suicide of the West, asserting that for a liberal there is no
enemy to the Left.

The four great intellectual influences on Bill Buckley were different in many ways, especially in temperament. But their similarities are telling. All were highly
educated—two of them, Kendall and Burnham, studied
at Oxford. Significantly, all were men of faith. Nock was a

onetime Episcopalian clergyman; Kendall was the son of a Methodist minister, and later converted to Catholicism; Chambers was an atheist who ultimately found solace as a Quaker; and Burnham was a lapsed Catholic who returned to the church in final days.

And most importantly, these four intellectuals—three of them formerly men of the Left—were united in their resolute opposition to the liberal zeitgeist. Buckley learned and borrowed freely from all of them throughout his life.

Standing Athwart History

The objective of the new magazine, Buckley wrote a prospective supporter, was "to revitalize the conservative position" and "influence the opinion-makers" of the nation. Buckley's use of the word *conservative* rather than *individualist,* the term he preferred in *God and Man at Yale* (published in 1951), underlines the profound impact of Russell Kirk's *The Conservative Mind* (published in 1953). Kirk's book gave the conservative movement its name and Buckley a cause to which he could rally conservatives of many different colors.

The challenge facing the new conservative magazine was enormous: the liberals had eight weekly journals of opinion, conservatives none (except for the *Human Events* newsletter). Liberals "know the power of ideas," Buckley said, "and it is largely for this reason that socialist-liberal forces have made such a great headway in the past thirty years."[11] The young editor took an openly elitist position, stating that his journal would attempt to appeal not to the grassroots but to conservative intellectuals and to those who "have midwifed and implemented the [socialist-liberal] revolution. We have got to have allies among [them]."[12]

In a memorandum for investors, Buckley called his publication "a formative journal" that would "change the nation's intellectual and political climate" just as the *Nation* and the *New Republic* helped usher in "the New Deal revolution." He conceded that it was a bold objective, but argued that the time was right for a magazine (and by implication a movement) that would oppose the growth of government, social engineers, and those who counseled coexistence with Communism, intellectual conformity, the elimination of the market economy, and world government.[13]

Framed in blue and type-heavy, with few illustrations, the first issue of *National Review* was dated November 19, 1955 (a week before editor-publisher William F. Buckley Jr.'s thirtieth birthday). It might have looked like just another right-wing journal, but its contents were anything but conventional.

The editors declared themselves to be "irrevocably" at war with "satanic" Communism—victory, not accommodation, must be the goal. They were unapologetically "libertarian" in the battle against the growth of government. They announced themselves to be "conservative" (that is, traditionalist) in the struggle between "the Social Engineers," who try to adjust mankind to scientific utopias, and "the disciples of Truth," who defend the "organic moral order." Surveying the world, Buckley trenchantly wrote that *National Review* "stands athwart history, yelling Stop."[14]

But it did so with a wink. The humor that abounded in the pages of the magazine set it apart from every other conservative journal of the time. In a cover article titled "How to Raise Money in the Ivy League," Aloise Buckley Heath explained that all one needs to do is to write a letter to fellow alumni warning them that "the best College in the World harbors pink professors." In "They'll Never Get Me on That Couch," Morrie Ryskind described the difficulties of Hollywood social life if you are (a) conservative and (b) unpsychoanalyzed.[15]

The magazine was deliberately eclectic, biographers Bridges and Coyne point out, making room for every strand of conservative thought—libertarians and Burkeans, free marketeers and Southern Agrarians, Madisonians and European monarchists. "The only categories excluded were racists, anti-Semites, and 'kooks.'"[16]

Prominent liberals did their best to belittle and bury the new journal. Murray Kempton in the *Progressive* called it a "national bore." Dwight Macdonald in *Commentary* wrote that the magazine appealed to "the half-educated, half-successful provincials . . . who responded to Huey Long, Father Coughlin, and Senator McCarthy." Of Buckley, he said condescendingly: "He would be an excellent journalist if he had a little more humor, common sense, and intellectual curiosity; also if he knew how to write." *Harper's* editor John Fischer saw deeper, more dangerous currents in the magazine, writing that *National Review* was not "an organ of conservatism, but of radicalism."[17]

The great majority of conservative intellectuals warmly welcomed the new journal on the block and lined up to write for it. A few declined, like the Southern agrarian Allen Tate, who did not share *National Review*'s enthusiasm for Senator McCarthy, and the Anglo-American poet

T. S. Eliot, who wrote Russell Kirk that the journal was "too consciously the vehicle of a defiant minority."[18] But in the words of the conservative historian George Nash, if *National Review* had not been founded, "there would probably have been no cohesive intellectual force on the Right in the 1960s and 1970s." Much of the history of American conservatism after 1955, Nash wrote, is the history of the individuals associated with the magazine William F. Buckley Jr. founded.[19]

The first print run was a modest 7,500. The average circulation remained less than 20,000 in its first three years, rising at last to 30,000 by 1960, its fifth anniversary. The magazine encountered frequent financial crises, and was forced in 1958 to become a biweekly. It remained afloat only because of an annual appeal by Buckley, who flouted all of the fundraising truisms—don't use long words, keep your letter to less than two pages, ask for money in the first paragraph, and keep asking for money through the P.S.

Buckley wrote as if to a friend about the ups and downs of the nation, the world, and the conservative movement before ending, almost as an afterthought, with an invitation to the reader to send along whatever he could to help sustain a publication that had become "the voice of American conservatism."[20] Several hundred thousand dollars was donated each year to *NR*—and they were not tax-deductible, because the magazine was a for-profit enterprise.

The largest individual donor to the magazine was William F. Buckley Jr., who in the years to come arranged for all of the income from his syndicated newspaper column, the *Firing Line* television program, book royalties, magazine and other articles, and lecture fees to be paid to

National Review. In exchange, *NR* paid Buckley a nominal salary and supplied him with a secretary and research assistance—sharing the latter expenses with *Firing Line*. How much did Buckley divert to *National Review* over fifty years? No one, not even the omnicompetent Frances Bronson, who "managed" Buckley for decades, has ever calculated precisely how much, but biographer Linda Bridges suggests, "It must have been in the millions of dollars."[21] An estimate of $200,000 a year for five decades, or a total gift of $10 million, does not seem unreasonable.

Throughout the 1950s and into the 1960s and 1970s and even beyond, Buckley spoke hundreds of times on college campuses, where his appearances became legend. One of the most notable was at Harvard, where in 1955 he debated the liberal newspaper editor James Wechsler. Jeffrey Hart, then stationed in the naval intelligence office in Boston, managed to find a seat in the packed auditorium. "All heads turned," Hart later wrote, "when Buckley and his wife Pat walked down the center aisle. She was tall, carried a leopard-skin bag and wore a large leopard-skin hat." She stole the show until Buckley's first remark: "I see Professor [Arthur] Schlesinger there in the third row. His books would be dangerous if they weren't so boring."

The Harvard students roared, loving the young conservative's chutzpah. On that evening, Hart wrote, it was very clear that here "was no boring, green-eyeshade Bob Taft conservatism" but a conservatism that was "intelligent, surprising, and fun." For the record, Buckley effortlessly bested Wechsler in the debate.[22]

Book publisher Jameson Campaigne Jr. recalls that, as a student at Williams College in Massachusetts in 1960, he invited Buckley to debate one of his deans before almost the entire college. After demolishing the dean during the formal debate, the still-fresh Buckley took on most of the Williams faculty during the question-and-answer period. "Buckley performed like 'Braveheart,'" says Campaigne, "lopping off the heads of one faculty lord and knight after another. . . . It was a devastating performance, an inspiration." For years, Campaigne received letters from fellow Williams graduates commenting on the memorable evening.[23]

Sometimes, particularly when a youth organization was involved, Buckley made other arrangements regarding his speaking fees. New York political activist Herb Stupp recalls that in 1971 Buckley lectured at St. John's University and Pace University, and then gave his honoraria to the schools' chapters of Young Americans for Freedom, a group Buckley helped found.[24]

The same year, Buckley came to Princeton to debate the ultraliberal Reverend William Sloane Coffin Jr. Jeff Greenfield, now a CBS News political correspondent, then a student activist, remembered how Buckley—"a man of incontestable assurance"—had suddenly appeared on a drab depressing downtown street alongside "an undergraduate flushed with excitement." Buckley, said Greenfield, was "put together entirely of angles—high cheekbones cutting inward to a sharp chin, a Roman nose, private school hair combed straight across a high forehead, and the most dexterous pair of eyebrows in the world." He was chatting animatedly with the student, "gesturing as forcefully as a Kennedy forefinger, the mouth pursing, exploding, collapsing again." One wonders, Greenfield said, "if

William F. Buckley Jr. notices the weary character of the street—one doubts it."[25]

An undemanding guest for the most part, Buckley had one inexorable rule: he had to be served a glass of wine or two prior to any evening lecture—it helped him relax, and besides, he was fond of wine of a good vintage. Early on in his public lecturing, he resolved to read his remarks from a prepared text rather than from notes or, God forbid, ad lib. "It requires experience to do this without appearing to be glued to the text," he explained in his book of collected speeches. "I have that experience." But he also insisted that there always be a question-and-answer period so he could satisfy the audience that "I can handle myself (and my interrogators) extemporaneously."[26]

Forty years after his first public appearance, Buckley was still visiting campuses and confronting liberal nostrums. As the 1993 Henry Salvatori Distinguished Lecturer of Young America's Foundation (the educational successor to Young Americans for Freedom), Buckley visited almost a dozen colleges from coast to coast, winding up at Williams College. Suffering from the flu, he canceled a planned Caribbean trip but insisted on completing his campus lectures.

Addressing an overflow crowd of twelve hundred at Williams, Buckley was obviously exhausted but nevertheless won an enthusiastic response from the audience with his witty analysis of Clinton's inaugural address, which he called "doublespeak." "Tricky Dick [Nixon] would have been run out of town with wet towels," he said, if he had been as deceitful as Clinton. Buckley quoted one line of the president's inaugural speech: "The American people have chosen the change we celebrate today." Examine that language, Buckley suggested, and what it says is, "I was elected president."[27] The same could be said about President Barack Obama.

A HANDS-ON EDITOR

In the first years—in fact until 1962, when he began writing a syndicated newspaper column—Bill Buckley devoted almost 100 percent of his working time to *National Review*. During this period he published only one book, *Up from Liberalism* (1959), in which he had the temerity to write that modern liberalism is more deserving of the label "reactionary" than modern conservatism. Modern liberals, he writes scornfully, believe that "truths are transitory and empirically determined," "equality is desirable and attainable through the action of state power," and "all peoples and societies should strive to organize themselves upon a rationalist and scientific paradigm." The conservative alternative, he says, calling on fusionist rhetoric, is based on "freedom, individuality, the sense of community, the sanctity of the family, the supremacy of the conscience, the spiritual view of life."[28]

"I will use *my* power as *I* see fit," he writes. "I mean to live my life an obedient man, but obedient to God, subservient to the wisdom of my ancestors; never to the authority of political truths arrived at yesterday at the voting booth." Such a program, concludes Buckley, "is enough to keep conservatives busy, and Liberals at bay. And the nation free."[29]

Buckley did everything at *National Review* but set the type. In the first year, he wrote more than half the editorials and a monthly column about education, "From the Ivory Tower." He chaired the weekly editorial meeting, at which articles and editorial ideas were debated and decided. He discovered gifted young writers like Garry Wills, Joan Didion, John Leonard, and Arlene Croce; among his later protégés were Richard Brookhiser, Linda Bridges, Mona Charen, Charles Kesler, Paul Gigot, Rich Lowry, and David Brooks. He also had the good sense to hire his sister Priscilla Buckley, a professional journalist, as managing editor. He knew he could depend upon Priscilla to produce a lively magazine if he was out of the office debating a wrongheaded liberal, writing a book, or sailing to Tahiti.

All the while, he insisted on enjoying himself and made sure that his *NR* confreres did the same. He hosted weekly lunches at Paone's; frequent dinners at his New York maisonette with his wife, Pat, as hostess; and most anticipated of all, the annual Christmas party at Wallacks Point in Stamford. For several years, the staff was treated to a performance of *The Messiah* at Carnegie Hall and then adjourned to the Buckley home for a lavish buffet.[30]

Editor Buckley clearly had certain goals in mind for his magazine: keep the Republican Party—the primary political vehicle of conservatives—tilted to the right; eliminate any and all extremists from the conservative movement; flay and fleece the liberals at every opportunity; and push hard for a policy of victory over Communism in the Cold War.

In pursuit of the first goal, *National Review* promoted Republican conservatives like Senator Barry Goldwater of Arizona, criticized "modern" Republicans like President

Dwight Eisenhower, and closely monitored philosophically shifty politicians like Richard Nixon.

In 1956, when considering whether to endorse Eisenhower for reelection, the editors began the debate by noting that Ike was not Adlai Stevenson, a predictable liberal
Democrat, or even Nelson Rockefeller, New York's big-
government Republican governor; and he was not a doctrinaire New Dealer or Fair Dealer. As Bridges and Coyne
put it, Ike "mostly didn't treat the taxpayer's money as if
it presumptively belonged to Washington."[31] In a signed
article, Buckley reluctantly agreed that the general was not
"an adventurer who would commit the nation's destiny in
pursuit of one beguiling horizon, or a redeemer cocksure
of his afflatus."

In October, the magazine published a two-man sym-
posium on the question "Should Conservatives Vote for
Eisenhower-Nixon?" Yes, said Burnham, ever the prag-
matist, because the Eisenhower administration was better
than the Democratic alternative on almost every point. No,
said Willi Schlamm, the idealist, because Eisenhower was
not a Republican but a Democratic president. The duty for
conservatives in this election, he argued, was "to break"
Eisenhower's control over the GOP.[32]

Four years later, there was another sharp debate among
senior editors, this time about whether to endorse Nixon
in the presidential race against John F. Kennedy. Eight
years of "a liberal Republican" in the White House, Frank
Meyer said, had "immensely weakened" the conservative
opposition in Congress and the states. Rather than endorsing Nixon, he said, the magazine should support Barry
Goldwater, whose emergence as a "principled conserva-

tive" gave the conservative movement a powerful "public symbol."[33] William A. Rusher, *NR* publisher since 1957 and a longtime GOP activist, argued that *National Review* would increase its leverage by not joining the Republican parade for Nixon.

Taking an endorse-Nixon position were James Burnham and Priscilla Buckley. A conservative, argued Burnham, "has to set his course within the frame of reality." And the reality was that those supporting John F. Kennedy were *National Review*'s "primary targets," including leftist ideologues, appeasers and collaborationists, socialists, fellow travelers, and Communists. The only meaningful way to declare against them in the election was to "vote for Nixon." Any "dodge," said Burnham, would be "a mistake, counter to *NR*'s best interests, and perhaps injurious to its future."[34]

Striving for a mean, Buckley announced in a signed editorial shortly before election day that the magazine would neither endorse a candidate nor recommend abstention. He listed the major arguments for each man, included a diligent disparagement of Kennedy, and concluded, disingenuously, that "*National Review* was not founded to make practical politics. Our job is to think, and write."[35]

But the magazine had, of course, been deeply involved in politics from its first issue. *National Review* had suggested Senator William Knowland of California as a presidential possibility if Eisenhower should not seek reelection. It had criticized the Eisenhower administration at every opportunity—for failing to respond in any serious way to the 1956 Hungarian Revolution and inviting the Soviet leader Nikita Khrushchev to the United States in 1959. Buckley was so outraged by the Khrushchev invitation that, with the help of the conservative impresario Marvin Liebman, he formed the Committee Against Summit Entanglements (CASE). He threatened to dye the Hudson River red so that when the Soviet dictator entered New York in 1960 to visit the United Nations, it would be on a "river of blood."[36]

In September, just a month before *National Review* said it was staying out of "practical politics," Buckley helped the conservative movement to take a big step into politics. He invited some one hundred conservative student activists to gather at Great Elm, the Buckley family estate in Sharon, Connecticut. This conference would mark the founding of Young Americans for Freedom (YAF). The group's founding statement, drafted by M. Stanton Evans, the twenty-six-year-old editor of the *Indianapolis News,* declared, "In this time of moral and political crises, it is the responsibility of the youth of America to affirm certain eternal truths." The "Sharon Statement," as it became known, affirmed the importance of limited government, the efficacy of the free market, and the need to seek victory over rather than coexistence with Communism—the very issues Buckley had made the focus of *National Review.*

There were two major debates among the young conservatives at Sharon: whether the phrase "the individual's use of his God-given free will" should be included in the founding statement, and whether they should call themselves "Young Americans for Freedom" or "Young Conservatives of America." The sticking point on the first question—at least for the libertarians present—was the G-word, "God." By a narrow vote of 44–40, "God-given free will" was retained. On the second question, pragma-

tists favored "Young Americans for Freedom," while pur-
ists preferred "Young Conservatives of America." Here
pragmatism prevailed, and by a healthy majority: "Young
Americans for Freedom" was adopted as the name of the
new conservative youth organization.[37]

"What is so striking in the students who met at Sharon," Buckley wrote, "is their appetite for power. Ten years
ago, the struggle seemed so long, so endless, even, that we
did not dream of victory. . . . It is quixotic to say that they or
their elders have seized the reins of history. But the difference in psychological attitude is tremendous."[38] A delighted
Buckley watched YAF go from triumph to triumph, holding mass rallies in New York City's Manhattan Center and
Madison Square Garden featuring Senator Barry Goldwater, challenging the National Student Association and other
liberal organizations on campus, and forcing the Firestone
Tire and Rubber Company to abandon its plan to build a
synthetic rubber plant in Communist Romania after YAF
threatened to hand out 500,000 leaflets condemning the
project at the Indianapolis 500 on Memorial Day. Later
Buckley and other older conservatives tried to help YAF
cope with infighting and financial mismanagement, but
the group eventually imploded. Still, YAF's achievements
were formidable, especially in Goldwater's 1964 presidential campaign, and demonstrated that conservatives could
make a difference in the political arena.

Another early political initiative of Buckley was the
Conservative Party of New York. In 1957, Buckley, philan-
thropist Jeremiah Milbank Jr., lawyer Thomas Bolan, and
several others met to discuss whether, in Buckley's words,
"the time [had] come to attempt to establish a counterpart

to the Liberal Party in New York." They believed that such
an outside conservative effort could move the Republican
Party to the right just as the Liberal Party had moved New
York's Democratic Party to the left and kept it there for
years.[39]

Buckley thought that Raymond Moley, a onetime FDR
brain-truster turned conservative columnist and author,
"would make an excellent chairman of the Conservative
Party."[40] It would take several years of discussion and planning, but these early meetings led to the founding of the
Conservative Party of New York in 1962 by two young,
dynamic Irish Catholic lawyers—Daniel Mahoney and
Kieran O'Doherty.

National Review became increasingly aggressive politically. In 1964 the magazine promoted enthusiastically
Barry Goldwater's candidacy for president. In 1965 Buckley
ran for mayor of New York City in a seemingly quixotic
campaign that would have far-reaching political consequences for the city and American conservatism. In 1968
NR endorsed Nixon over Vice President Hubert Humphrey,
reflecting the ever more intimate coupling of the conservative movement and the Republican Party.

But while working within the mainstream political system, conservatives were also building an effective, prudential counterestablishment. Careful to protect the advances
that had been made, Buckley acted decisively when he saw
it necessary to dissociate the conservative movement from
the irresponsible Right.

The first prominent extremist read out of the movement was the objectivist author Ayn Rand, an action
occasioned in part by Rand's growing influence among

young conservatives. When Buckley first met Rand, her first words to him, heavily accented by her native Russian tongue, were, "You ahrr too intelligent to believe in Gott." For the next two or three years, Buckley sent the Russian-born writer postcards in liturgical Latin. "But levity with Miss Rand was not an effective weapon," he later wrote—stronger measures were called for.[41]

In December 1957, Whittaker Chambers took up arms against the neo-Nietzschean founder of objectivism and her 1,168-page novel, *Atlas Shrugged*. Reviewing the book in *National Review*, Chambers declared that its story was preposterous, its characters crude caricatures, its message "dictatorial." Although Rand insisted she was antistatist, Chambers wrote, she called for a society run by a "techno-cratic elite." "Out of a lifetime of reading," he said, "I can recall no other book in which a tone of overriding arro-gance was so implacably sustained."[42]

Chambers was joined by other prominent conserva-tives. Russell Kirk called objectivism a false and detestable "inverted religion." Frank Meyer accused Rand of "calcu-lated cruelties" and the presentation of an "arid subhuman image of man." Garry Wills called Rand a "fanatic." A furious Rand described *National Review* as "the worst and most dangerous magazine in America," and vowed never again to remain in the same room with Bill Buckley, a promise she kept.[43]

A few years later, in an essay on conservatism, Buckley elaborated on the reasons for Rand's exclusion. It was in part, he wrote, the result of "her desiccated philosophy's conclusive incompatibility with the conservative's empha-sis on transcendence, intellectual and moral." There was also her tone, he said, "that hard, schematic, implacable, unyielding dogmatism that is in itself intrinsically objectionable," whether from Savonarola or Rand.[44]

Buckley treated laissez-faire economist Murray Rothbard and "his merry anarchists" more gently, but no less firmly, stating that their antistatism collided with conservatives who recognize that the state "sometimes is, and is today as never before, the necessary instrument of proximate deliverance" from Communism. When a Rothbardian charged that *National Review* was betraying its own principles, Buckley responded that it was not sane to equate the repeal of Social Security and the containment of the Soviet Union. "The problem of assigning priorities to the two objectives," he said, "is not merely a problem of intellectual discrimination, but of moral balance."[45]

In the same essay, Buckley also dealt with God. Can you be a conservative and believe in God? he asked. Obviously. "Can you be a conservative and not believe in God?" "This is an empirical essay," he said, "and so the answer is, as obviously, yes." Then he raised the bar. "Can you be a conservative and despise God and feel contempt for those who believe in God? I would say no." He differentiated between the agnostic who "can shrug his shoulders about the whole thing," the atheist "who knows there is no God, but doesn't much care about those who disagree," and the God hater who "regards those who believe or tolerate religion as afflicted with short-circuited vision."[46]

THE PURGE

By mid-1961, conservatism was becoming a discernible presence in American politics. It was manifested in the bestsellerdom of *The Conscience of a Conservative* by Barry Goldwater (and L. Brent Bozell), the increased circulation of *National Review* and *Human Events,* Republican John Tower's upset victory in Texas to fill Lyndon Johnson's Senate seat (Johnson having been elected vice president in 1960), and the accelerating activities of Young Americans for Freedom.

Liberals had generally ignored the conservative upsurge, but were now driven to denounce and attempt to inter it. Liberal politicians, academics, columnists, clerics, and even humorists like Jack Paar used their various skills, creating what Buckley called "the echo-chamber effect."[47]

Such blowback threatened the progress that Buckley and other leaders had made in advancing conservatism as a political force. Of particular concern to Buckley was the John Birch Society. Founded in late 1958 by Robert Welch, the society focused zealously on the Communist menace at home and abroad, quickly establishing a sizable presence in conservative states like California, Arizona, and Texas. While Buckley was fiercely anti-Communist, he viewed Welch's ideas as "wild" and irrational. Welch had, for instance, said that Dwight Eisenhower was a "dedicated, conscious agent of the Communist conspiracy." "The true cause of our present imminent danger," Welch said more than once, is "a semi-secret international cabal whose members sit in the highest places of influence and power worldwide."[48]

Buckley saw that such extremism would harm the anti-Communist cause to which he was so passionately committed. He determined that Welch must be cast out of the conservative movement—a self-conscious decision endorsed by the majority of conservatives who looked to *National Review* for intellectual leadership. But this expulsion would prove more difficult than Rand's because: (1) several senior editors argued that the magazine should concentrate its fire on Communists and liberals, not other conservatives; and (2) no one was quite certain of the immediate economic consequences to the magazine. How many subscribers would cancel their subscriptions? Would any advertisers pull their ads? To Buckley, however, Welch's ejection was a necessary action and part of the discriminating fusionism he was creating.

Over the objections of editors Brent Bozell, Frank Meyer, and William Rickenbacker and publisher William Rusher, Buckley wrote an extended editorial expelling Welch from the conservative movement. Supported by Burnham and his sister Priscilla, Buckley declared that Welch was "damaging the cause of anti-Communism" with his inability to make the critical distinction between an "active pro-Communist" and an "ineffectually anti-Communist Liberal." Buckley said scornfully that Welch's scoreboard describing the United States as "50–70 percent Communist-controlled" was in effect saying that "the government of the United States is under operational control of the Communist Party." The editorial concluded that "love of truth and country called for the firm rejection of Welch's false counsels."[49]

Some subscribers who were John Birch Society members angrily canceled their subscriptions, as Rusher had warned they would, but the great majority of readers agreed with Senators Tower and Goldwater, both of whom wrote letters to the editor endorsing the magazine's stand. They understood that rather than dividing the conservative cause, Buckley had strengthened it and saluted him for his courage and leadership. One letter to the editor read: "You have once again given a voice to the conscience of conservatism." It was signed, "Ronald Reagan, Pacific Palisades, Cal."[50]

Buckley also took a firm stand against anti-Semitism by informing *National Review*'s writers in April 1959 that the magazine would "not carry on its masthead the name of any person whose name also appears on the masthead of the *American Mercury*." Under owner Russell Maguire, the latter magazine had descended into the foul-smelling swamps of neo-Nazism, endorsing the theory of a worldwide Jewish conspiracy set forth in the fraudulent *Protocols of Zion*.[51]

Nearly thirty years later, Buckley would publish *In Search of Anti-Semitism* (1992), described by Jeffrey Hart as "one of his best books." The greater part of the work had first appeared in *National Review* in December 1991. *In Search of Anti-Semitism,* Hart said, performed delicate surgery necessary "to the process of shaping the American conservative mind." The growth that required excision was "a neoisolationist nativism tinged with anti-Semitism" set forth by paleoconservative columnists Joseph Sobran and Patrick Buchanan and the paleo journal *Chronicles*.[52] In his introduction to the book, *National Review* editor John O'Sullivan points out that since its founding, the magazine "has quietly played the role of conscience of the Right," removing the cranks when necessary "from the ranks of respectable conservatism."[53]

Neoconservative Norman Podhoretz demanded Sobran's and Buchanan's excommunication from the conservative movement, but Buckley would not accede to so drastic a sentence. Instead, as biographers Bridges and Coyne report, Buckley wrote that Sobran and Buchanan were not anti-Semitic in any normal sense of the word but were anti-Israel, which colored their views about U.S. foreign policy. Referring to the first Gulf War, Buchanan wrote, "The only two groups that are beating the drum for war in the Middle East [are] the Israeli Defense Ministry and its amen corner in the United States."[54]

Buckley's criticism did not come easily: Sobran had been a popular senior editor of *National Review* and colleague of Buckley for two decades. Buchanan had been a brilliant polemicist for conservatism since the 1960s and made a strong populist run for the Republican presidential nomination in 1992. But the man who had led the conservative movement out of the wilderness and into a position of intellectual and political prominence could not remain silent about an issue that might materially damage American conservatism. As important was the simple fact that anti-Semitism was morally wrong.

More than a year later, Sobran wrote a long essay titled "How I Was Fired by Bill Buckley," in which he argued that the Buckley conservatism he knew and admired in the 1960s and the 1970s—"a politics appropriate to the tradition of Aquinas, Dante, Shakespeare, and Dr. Johnson"— was no more. *National Review,* he said, had become "a neoconservative magazine" with "no real separate existence from that of *Commentary* or *The Public Interest*."

The estrangement continued until late 2006 when it was reported that Buckley had checked into the Mayo Clinic for treatment of his severe emphysema. After a decade of silence, Joe Sobran published a sympathetic column titled "The Real Bill Buckley." He recounted Buckley's many acts of generosity and charity, which "went far beyond sharing his money." He described how Buckley stayed with an old Yale friend to comfort him when his small daughter died of brain cancer. "What a great heart," Sobran wrote, "eager to spread joy, and ready to share grief." The political differences that "drove us apart seem trivial now," he said. "I learned a lot of things from Bill Buckley, but the best thing he taught me was how to be a Christian."[55]

American Jews recognized Buckley's signal contribution. Jonathan Tobin, a contributor to the *Jewish World Review* and executive editor of the *Philadelphia Jewish Exponent*, wrote that "as much as any other person, Bill Buckley cleared the way not only for a conservative movement where Jews would be welcomed," but "set the stage for an American politics in which anti-Semitism was confined to the fever swamps of the far right and far left."[56]

NR and its editor did not acquit themselves as well on the issue of civil rights in the 1950s and early 1960s, taking a states' rights position that equaled, in the eyes of most liberals and almost all black Americans, a stand in favor of segregation and therefore racism. In his articles, Buckley clearly rejected the politics of southern racists like Ross Barnett of Mississippi and George Wallace of Alabama, but he also argued that the federal enforcement of integration was worse than the *temporary* continuation of segregation. Consistent with conservative principles, he favored voluntary gradual change.

But Mississippi was burning, and freedom riders were being murdered. You were either for civil rights or against them, declared blacks who did not see a dime's worth of difference between Wallace and Buckley. As a result of *NR*'s above-the-fray philosophizing and Barry Goldwater's vote, on constitutional grounds, against the Civil Rights Act of 1964, the albatross of racism was hung around the neck of American conservatism and remained there for decades, and even to the present.

In the late 1960s, Buckley and other conservative intellectuals began to change their position about race in America. During a 1968 teachers' strike, Buckley wrote that it was "racist" to appoint a black teacher because he was black, but he added that America had reached "a point in race relations where it becomes desirable . . . to accede to such demands of the Negro community as are in the least way plausible. Negro control over the education of Negro children would appear to be one of those defensible objectives."[57]

In a panel discussion marking *NR*'s fiftieth anniversary in October 2005, liberal commentator Jeff Greenfield asked Buckley whether he regretted his own and the magazine's resistance to the civil rights movement. Yes, Buckley replied, he realized that in retrospect he and his colleagues were relying too much on normal political processes as outlined in the Constitution to fully incorporate blacks into American public life. Many southern states, he admitted, simply did not permit blacks to participate.[58]

A contributing factor to the magazine's position was that many black activists, including Martin Luther King Jr., were allied with the far Left. Bill Rusher was aware, from his work with the Senate Subcommittee on Internal Security, that two of King's closest associates, Stanley Levison and Hunter Pitts (Jack) O'Dell, were ranking members of the Communist Party. But such associations did not justify *National Review*'s consistent refusal to concede the reality of the racism and its attendant horrors that prevailed throughout the Deep South.

FUSIONISM

One other important task had to be accomplished in this early period before the conservative movement could be a major player in American politics: it had to be philosophically united. Throughout the 1950s, traditionalists and libertarians snapped and snarled at each other in *National Review* and elsewhere. Traditionalist Russell Kirk was accused of being hostile to individualism and laissez-faire economics, while libertarian F. A. Hayek was faulted for defending freedom on strictly utilitarian grounds rather than according to "the absolute transcendent values upon which its strength is founded."[59]

One conservative was convinced that beneath the fierce rhetoric lay a true consensus of principle. Frank Meyer was the fast-talking, chain-smoking, ex-Communist senior editor of *NR*. Through articles, books, and endless late-evening telephone calls, Meyer communicated his synthesis of the disparate elements of conservatism that came to be called fusionism (a word coined not by Meyer but by traditionalist Brent Bozell, who did not think that any lasting correlation of freedom and virtue was possible).[60]

The core of conservatism, Meyer said, was "the freedom of the person, the central and primary end of political society." The state had only three limited functions, according to Meyer: national defense, the preservation of domestic order, and the administration of justice between citizens. The "achievement of virtue" was not a political question; indeed, it was not even the state's business. Freedom, Meyer argued, was the indispensable condition for the pursuit of virtue. Freedom was the ultimate *political* end; virtue was the ultimate end of man as man.

But as John Adams wrote, "Public virtue is the only foundation of republics." There must be "a positive passion for the public good" established in the minds of the people, Adams said, or there can be "no republican government, nor any real liberty."[61]

Meyer insisted that modern American conservatism was not classical liberalism, which had been significantly weakened by utilitarianism and secularism. Most classical liberals, he said, were seemingly unable to distinguish between "the *authoritarianism*" of the state and "the *authority* of God and truth." Meyer said that conservatives were trying to save the Christian understanding of "the nature and destiny of man."[62] To do that, they had to absorb the best of *both* branches of the divided conservative mainstream. Meyer insisted that he was not creating something new but simply articulating an already existing conservative consensus, the consensus forged so brilliantly by the founding fathers in 1787 in the writing of the Constitution.

Regardless of their philosophical orientation, the historian George Nash observes, all conservatives thought the state should be circumscribed and were deeply suspicious of planning and attempts to centralize power. They defended the Constitution "as originally conceived" and opposed the "messianic" Communist threat to Western civilization.[63]

Striving as ever for consensus, Buckley suggested in an essay titled "Notes Toward an Empirical Definition of Conservatism" that what *National Review* had striven to do from the beginning was to achieve "a general consensus on the proper balance between freedom, order, justice, and tradition."[64] As Buckley might have put it, "Fusionism, anyone?"

Flaying the Left

While pushing the GOP to the right and building a prudential conservative movement, Buckley steadily pursued the other objectives he had laid out for himself and his magazine. Consistent with the third goal, *NR* kept impaling liberals. President John F. Kennedy, for example, was a frequent target in Buckley's newly launched newspaper column, "On the Right." When Kennedy settled the Cuban missile crisis in October 1962 by promising not to invade the island in exchange for the removal of Soviet missiles, Buckley wrote that the president had "formally given our bitterest enemy a pledge that we will enforce the nonenforcement of the Monroe Doctrine!"[65] The syndicated column was a milestone in Buckley's career, enabling him to reach not just the self-selected people who came to a debate or bought a book or subscribed to *National Review* but a national readership.[66]

Buckley continued to take on liberals in venues across the country, averaging as many as seventy lectures a year. In a debate with the novelist Norman Mailer, Buckley remarked, "The American right wing, of whom I am merely one member, [is] clumsily trying to say what Norman Mailer with his superior skills would be saying so very much better if only he would raise his eyes from the world's genital glands."[67]

When Harvard historian and Kennedy adviser Arthur Schlesinger Jr. debated Buckley in January 1961, he tried to set up his conservative opponent with an extravagant compliment: "Mr. Buckley has a facility for rhetoric which I envy as well as a wit which I seek clumsily and vainly to emulate." Buckley got his revenge by using the Schlesinger quote as a blurb for his new anthology, *Rumbles Left and Right*. A furious Schlesinger threatened to sue, and the publisher suggested removing the blurb. Buckley insisted it be kept, promising to pay the damages in case the Harvard professor won. But that was not all. When Buckley met Schlesinger at a party, he drawled, "Your deadline for my next cover blurb is the first of the month." Schlesinger went ballistic.[68]

The final objective—the defeat of Communism—was the cause that aroused Buckley more than any other and inspired his most searing rhetoric. To Buckley, Robert Welch's wild conspiracy theories were especially damaging because they deflected public attention from the establishment's flabby response to the Communist threat. Buckley documented how *New York Times* reporter Herbert Matthews assiduously promoted and covered up for Fidel Castro. Matthews had insisted in a front-page article that Castro was not a Communist, not "under Communist influence," and not even a dupe of Communism. There are, Matthews stated flatly, "no Communists in positions of control" in Cuba. Buckley titled his article "Herbert Matthews and Fidel Castro: I Got My Job Through the *New York Times*."[69]

Regarding the nonresponse of the United States to the Soviet crushing of the Hungarian Revolution, Buckley wrote: "For a few stunning days, early in November in 1956, the freedom fighters of Budapest held the entire Communist world at bay. America was struck by the intensity—and efficacy—of the anti-Communist spirit, and we were breathless with wonder and admiration. But in the end, we did nothing. 'For a while,' Mr. Eugene Lyons, a wise and veteran American anti-Communist, remarked to me, 'it looked almost as though Budapest would liberate the United States.'"[70]

The Voice

On the occasion of *National Review*'s fifth anniversary, Buckley listed the certitudes that conservatives shared, starting with: "The Communist experiment [is] the worst abuse of freedom in history" and "the socialized state is to justice, order, and freedom what the Marquis de Sade is to love."[71]

His comments were delivered at a glittering black-tie dinner in the Plaza Hotel's ornate Grand Ballroom hosted by former president Herbert Hoover, General Douglas MacArthur, and Admiral Lewis Strauss, the former chairman of the Atomic Energy Commission—a program calculated to demonstrate that the magazine had not only survived the critical first years of publication but had become *the* voice of a burgeoning intellectual and political movement.

Much had been achieved and much had changed at the magazine. Among those no longer on the masthead were Willi Schlamm, who had resigned in a fit of pique when Buckley tired of his overbearing attitude toward him and everyone else on the magazine and asked him to limit his contributions to social and cultural commentary; Brent Bozell, who moved his family to Spain so he could finish his book on the Warren Court and consider whether he should start a conservative Catholic magazine; and Willmoore Kendall—philosophically sound but personally impossible—who resigned from both Yale and *NR* and joined the faculty of a new and very Catholic school, the University of Dallas. Even Buckley the master diplomat could not effect a rapprochement with Kendall, the ultimate contrarian.

Although declining to support Nixon, Buckley regarded Kennedy's presidential victory as a setback for conservatives. At the fifth-anniversary dinner, he reiterated, Nock-like, the responsibility of the magazine to nurture a Remnant of conservative ideas. "We are probably destined," he said, "to live out our lives in something less than a totally harmonious relationship with our times." Nevertheless, Buckley added, we can all take comfort in knowing "that for so long as it is mechanically possible, you have a journal, a continuing witness to those truths which animated the birth of our country, and continue to animate our lives."[72]

CHAPTER 3

CRUISING SPEED

In the 1960s, American conservatism experienced spectacular political growth, nominating one of its own—Senator Barry Goldwater—for president, and electing an equally unapologetic conservative—Ronald Reagan—as governor of the second-most-populous state in the union. Central to these political successes was the omnipresence of Bill Buckley as hands-on editor, bestselling author, incisive columnist, rapier-witted television host, unparalleled debater, and not-so-quixotic candidate for mayor of the most liberal city in America—New York City. In his spare time, he skied in Switzerland, sailed from Newport to Bermuda and eventually across the Atlantic, and partied with friends on the Right and the Left such as John Kenneth Galbraith, Henry Kissinger, Clare Boothe Luce, Tom Wolfe, and Alistair Cooke.

He even took up painting, although with less than laudable results. At Gstaad, Switzerland, Buckley's friend

David Niven brought the famous French artist Marc Chagall to visit the chateau the Buckleys rented every winter. Over Niven's objections, Buckley immediately took Chagall to his studio. Chagall looked at Buckley's paintings, picked up a tube of paint, and said in French, "The poor paint!"[1]

His cruising speed violated all normal limits. Once asked why he worked so hard and didn't take life easier, he replied, "I am easily bored."[2] But in reality he was honoring the injunctions of his father and of Edward Pulling, founder of the Millbrook School, to repay his country for the bountiful patrimony it had bequeathed him.

One thing he did not do during this period was to write a "big book" providing his understanding of the conservative philosophy—something he had talked of doing for several years, following the publication of *Up from Liberalism* in 1959. The book was tentatively called *The Revolt Against the Masses*, a play on the title of the Spanish conservative Ortega y Gasset's classic work, *The Revolt of the Masses*. Buckley would show that a conservative revolt against the masses—that is, against Marxism—was in the making.

He had developed a routine of going to Gstaad for six or eight weeks every winter to write the first draft of a book. But when he set out to write *The Revolt Against the Masses* in Switzerland in the first part of 1964, he struggled. After a month of thought and work, he had produced only ten thousand not particularly riveting words.

Buckley later diagnosed his problem with *Revolt*: his thesis no longer seemed to apply. He had expected America "to realize that it has to go back to serious thought, and away from these distracting frivolities with which we had been preoccupied. Exactly the opposite happened. Instead of going against the masses, we went right into a situation where the masses tyrannized—the Berkeley campus blowup."[3] (In late 1964 thousands of student protestors seized control of the Berkeley administration building.)

More to the point, all his biographers agree, is that Bill Buckley admitted to himself that he was not a political philosopher but a popularizer of ideas. His responsibility to himself and to the movement he was shaping was to apply the scholars' findings to prevailing problems and to disseminate their ideas as widely as possible through "the force of his personality as well as the written word," as Linda Bridges and John Coyne write.[4] His friend Hugh Kenner, who urged him to write *Revolt*, thought that Buckley "was already moving too fast to do anything but the topical." Buckley accepted the assessment of his colleague William Rickenbacker: "He knows he's quick, but doubts he's deep."[5] Author-editor M. Stanton Evans, a longtime *NR* contributor, thought that Buckley could be a philosopher if he put his mind to it, but instead he concentrated on acting "as a broker and analyst of ideas, rather than as an originator of them."[6]

There was no question that Buckley could be a deeply moving writer. Typical was the unsigned editorial he wrote following John Kennedy's assassination on November 22, 1963. As Americans of all parties and pursuits mourned the violent death of the young president, Buckley wrote: "The grief was spontaneous and, in most cases, wholly sincere. Not because Mr. Kennedy's policies were so universally beloved, but because he was a man so intensely charming, whose personal vigor and robust enjoyment of life so invigorated almost all who beheld him."[7]

Much the same could be said of Bill Buckley—and was, following his death.

THE GOLDWATER CAMPAIGN

The political climax of conservatism in the 1960s was Goldwater's historic presidential campaign. Among the reasons for Goldwater's ascendancy were his bestselling manifesto *The Conscience of a Conservative* (ghostwritten by L. Brent Bozell); Richard Nixon's deliberately moderate and losing presidential campaign in 1960; Governor Nelson Rockefeller's abrupt fall from Republican grace after divorcing his wife of thirty-some years and marrying his former secretary; President John F. Kennedy's mounting problems with southern Democrats and other factions within the Democratic Party; and a growing unease among the general public that America was not doing all it could do to defeat Communism. Goldwater offered sharp-edged conservative solutions, such as seeking victory rather than accommodation in the Cold War and rolling back government rather than managing it more efficiently, as modern Republicans sought to do.

In the 1964 Goldwater campaign, George Nash points out, politics and ideas were related as they "had not been for a long time." *National Review* happily promoted Goldwater's candidacy. Russell Kirk helped draft several of his speeches, including a major address at Notre Dame, and frequently praised him in his syndicated newspaper column. Professor Harry Jaffa of Ohio State University wrote Goldwater's acceptance speech at the Republican National

Convention. Milton Friedman, among other conservative academics, served as an economic adviser. "It is likely," Nash writes, "that without the patient spadework of the intellectual Right, the conservative *political* movement of the 1960s would have remained disorganized and defeated."[8]

Not everyone at *National Review*, however, welcomed the Goldwater candidacy. James Burnham had doubts about the senator's intellectual capacity and regarded his "why not victory?" policy to end the Cold War as simplistic. Burnham suggested Rockefeller at editorial meetings as a possible alternative. The suggestion precipitated cries of horror from Frank Meyer and William Rusher, who pointed to Governor Rockefeller's bloated New York state budgets and his exclusion of conservatives from his administration and among his top advisers. If Goldwater won the nomination, they argued, the Republican Party would advance significantly toward becoming the conservative party. If Goldwater did not win the presidency, they said, conservatives would still be able to point to his nomination as proof that American conservatism had become a political force to be reckoned with. Rusher was not a disinterested observer; along with political tactician F. Clifton White and Representative John Ashbrook of Ohio, he was a prime mover in the draft-Goldwater movement.

Buckley, affected by Burnham's realpolitik arguments, was more cautious about Goldwater, but he was attracted to Goldwater's libertarian views on government ("I did not come to Washington to pass laws but to repeal them," the senator declared in *The Conscience of a Conservative*) and his uncompromising anti-Communism. Biographer

John Judis links Buckley and Burnham in a deep skepticism about Goldwater, but Buckley participated in two private high-level meetings—one in Palm Beach, the other in Washington, D.C.—at which he sought an advisory position in the Goldwater campaign. Both meetings were coordinated by Jay Gordon Hall, a Washington lobbyist with a Ph.D., who had befriended Goldwater shortly after his first senatorial victory in 1952 and had done research and some speechwriting for the senator ever since.

In the end, Buckley's proposal at the September 1963 meeting to form a group of leading academics who would counsel Goldwater on public policy was blocked by the man who already had the senator's ear and was determined to share it with no one else—William Baroody, the president (on leave) of the American Enterprise Institute. Although Goldwater later claimed that he would have welcomed them, Buckley, Brent Bozell, and Bill Rusher were all prevented from making any significant contribution to the 1964 campaign. The Goldwater team even barred Buckley from speaking at a Young Americans for Freedom rally at the Republican National Convention in San Francisco, although he had been listed as a main speaker and the organization had been founded at his family's home.

Throughout 1964, Buckley weighed Goldwater's candidacy in terms of how its success or failure would affect the future of the conservative movement. In late May, he said at a *National Review* editorial meeting that if Goldwater lost the upcoming California primary, the magazine should urge him to withdraw from the race to prevent a humiliating defeat at the national convention. His analysis was based on a shaky premise. If asked, F. Clifton White would have told Buckley that Goldwater had enough delegates locked up to win on the first ballot, regardless of how he fared in California.[9]

After Goldwater narrowly won the Republican primary in California, Buckley attempted to prepare fellow conservatives for the inevitable outcome in the general election, writing, "This is probably Lyndon Johnson's year, and the Archangel Gabriel running on the Republican ticket probably couldn't win."[10] He was correct: every poll, public and private, had been saying all year that the American people wanted President Johnson to carry out the martyred Kennedy's program. They were not interested in having a third president in one year, whether it was Goldwater, Rockefeller, Henry Cabot Lodge, William Scranton, Nixon, or any other Republican.

But sometimes you win by losing. Goldwater's presidential bid enabled him to raise issues and propose conservative solutions to those issues; to forge a national political organization that would be used by future conservative candidates; to establish for conservatives a broad financial base stemming from direct mail and television appeals; and to demonstrate that a political force called conservatism could nominate a conservative and capture millions of votes. All of this went far beyond the original Buckley cry of trying to *stop* history and entered a new realm of attempting to *shape* history.

Buckley persisted in his public warnings that Goldwater's chances were hopeless, telling the delegates to YAF's annual convention in September—two months before election day—to prepare themselves for "the impending defeat of Barry Goldwater." Young conservatives looking for a rallying cry received instead the bleak advice that all they could do was to prepare for future Novembers—"if there is a future."[11] Fearing a chilling effect on political activity, YAF national chairman Robert Bauman forbade distribution of Buckley's remarks to the news media.

A month later, at the anniversary dinner of the Conservative Party of New York, Buckley took a different tack, mentioning Goldwater only once and focusing on what conservatives might accomplish in the next decades. He spoke of the possible and the ideal in politics. "How this movement, considering the contrary tug of history," he said, "has got as far as it has got, is something that surpasses the understanding of natural pessimists like myself."[12]

Buckley argued that if conservatives in politics wanted to be successful they had to steer a middle course between the ideal and the prudential. This golden mean, inspired by Burnham and Chambers (who had died in 1961), became Bill Buckley's guiding principle and would, in Judis's words, "influence a great many conservative politicians."[13]

But the golden mean is not a precise midway point between two extremes; rather, it is a shifting point that sometimes winds up closer to the ideal, sometimes closer to the prudential. Buckley would veer between the two, depending upon the issue and the state of the conservative movement, in the years ahead.

In spite of the overwhelming Goldwater defeat—he received only 38.5 percent of the popular vote and carried just six states—Buckley was not demoralized. Along with T. S. Eliot, he believed that there are no permanent defeats because there are no permanent victories. Buckley immediately sent a telegram to Goldwater, stating: "I wish to express my gratitude as an American for the gallant work you did for all your countrymen. I have no doubt at all that history will one day reward you."[14]

He also took concrete action to strengthen the conservative movement. He agreed in December 1964 to serve on the board of directors of a new political organization for "senior" conservatives—the American Conservative Union, best known in later years for the annual Conservative Political Action Conference (CPAC) that attracts thousands of participants. The same month he helped form, along with Milton Friedman, the Philadelphia Society, an association of conservative intellectuals modeled after the free-market Mont Pelerin Society. He put up the first $100 for the society's bank account, and over the next decade contributed an estimated $50,000 to the society through his share of a trust fund.[15]

He was always responsive when young people came calling. David Jones, the energetic executive director of Young Americans for Freedom, saw the need for an educational counterpart to YAF. Former New Jersey governor Charles Edison agreed to lend his name to the new organization, which became the Charles Edison Youth Fund (later the Fund for American Studies). When Jones asked Buckley to serve as the founding chairman, he declined, citing his commitments to *National Review,* but he joined the board of trustees and was a frequent speaker at the fund's events. In September 1998, he gave the keynote address at the fund's dinner honoring Jones, who had recently died. Buckley confessed his open admiration for Jones and the fund's efforts through its institutes at Georgetown University and overseas to teach rising young leaders about economic and political freedom.

Shortly after the Goldwater defeat, Buckley invited the gifted political operative F. Clifton White to dine with him in his Manhattan apartment to discuss the campaign. White was amazed that he did 90 percent of the talking. "He wanted to know exactly what I had done to get the Goldwater nomination and how I had done it. . . . He decided it must be something significant and worthwhile."[16]

Buckley may have been considering his next political act, which would complete his transformation into one of the most celebrated public figures, left or right, in America. Whatever his course or his trajectory, he never abandoned the magazine he had founded or the movement he had fashioned, but took them along on an increasingly breathtaking ride.

BUCKLEY FOR MAYOR?

In early 1965, Ronald Reagan was considering whether he should seek the Republican nomination for governor of California. When approached to run, he responded, "I'm an actor, not a politician." But he admitted that the public reaction to his October 1964 telecast for Barry Goldwater had exceeded anything in his movie or television career. The title of his 1963 autobiography (borrowed from his dramatic hospital bed scene in the film *King's Row*) was *Where's the Rest of Me?* Was it possible, the fifty-four-year-old actor asked himself, that he would find the answer in politics?

Three thousand miles away, the forty-year-old Bill

Buckley was mulling over whether to run for mayor of— what else?—New York City.

There were several reasons why he was eyeing the New York City mayoralty. First, he wanted to help block the rapid rise of Congressman John Lindsay, the golden boy of liberal Republicans. Lindsay's backers planned to move their man up the political ladder from congressman to mayor to governor to president of the United States. Such a succession was a prospect devoutly rejected by all right-thinking citizens.

Second, the conservative movement could use a political boost after the Goldwater defeat, and a good showing by a conservative candidate in the center of liberalism would do just that.

Third, Buckley had some ideas about the conduct of a large city's affairs (borrowed heavily from Harvard professors Nathan Glazer and Daniel Patrick Moynihan) that merited serious public discussion. Where better to have that discussion than in New York City, headquarters of the nation's news media?

Finally, running for mayor of New York would be fun and anything but boring, the one thing on God's earth that Buckley could not abide. Besides, he knew he would get a book out of the experience.

Although he insisted at the time—and later in *The Unmaking of a Mayor,* his witty account of his campaign— that the conservative movement was not a factor in his decision to run, Buckley was being either disingenuous or naïve. In the year 1965, you could no more separate Buckley and American conservatism than you could uncouple the pope and Roman Catholicism.

Looking back on this critical event in the history of the conservative movement, John O'Sullivan, who would in time succeed Buckley as editor of *National Review,* wrote, "Bill knew that if conservatism had any future, it had to be a hard political movement as well as a soft intellectual movement. It also had to have appeal to people other than *NR* subscribers. And it had to succeed—or at least be protected from failure. So WFB launched a serious bid for the New York mayoralty disguised as a lark."[17]

In early June, and not yet a candidate, Buckley wrote a column titled "Mayor, Anyone?" that set forth a ten-point platform on which a candidate might run. What strikes the reader is how libertarian it is. He recommended that "anti-narcotic laws for adults" be repealed, gambling be legalized, anyone without a police record be allowed to operate a car as a taxi, and communities be encouraged to finance their own "watchmen," relieving the municipal police force of what he called "an almost impossible job."[18] In these proposals we see the invisible hand of Albert Jay Nock, a continuing intellectual influence on Buckley.

The would-be mayoral candidate also displayed formidable prescience. He anticipated Representative Jack Kemp's enterprise-zone proposal of a decade later by suggesting that state and federal authorities suspend property and income taxes for all "Negro or Puerto Rican entrepreneurs" who established businesses in depressed areas in the inner city. And he proposed, several years before Governor Reagan offered his hard-nosed welfare-reform program in California, that all welfare recipients be required to do "street cleaning and general prettification work" for the city. Here was the first conservative enunciation of the workfare principle, or as Buckley put it rather crudely, "No workee, no dolee."[19]

The *New York Times* dismissed Buckley's formal announcement as an "exercise in futility," and predicted that New York voters would reject Buckley's "kind of Republicanism" as decisively as the nation had repudiated "Goldwaterism." Buckley quickly responded with a letter to the editor listing the reforms the *Times* had not mentioned in its news story: an increase in the police force; lower taxes; workfare; a disavowal of those who "encourage racism, lawlessness, and despair" among blacks; decentralization of city schools; and a reduction of the urban renewal and city planning that were "dehumanizing" New York City.[20]

Although serious about his proposals, Buckley, the candidate of the Conservative Party of New York, harbored no illusions about his chances. Asked at a news conference what he would do if he were elected, Buckley delivered the most quoted line of the campaign, and perhaps his life: "Demand a recount."

The widely viewed television debates between Conservative Buckley, Republican John Lindsay, and Democrat Abe Beame were devastating for Lindsay, revealing his superficiality, short temper, and just plain dullness. In contrast, Buckley was always ready with a bon mot. In one debate, the moderator advised the conservative candidate that he had "another moment if you care to comment." Buckley replied with a smile, "No, I think I'll just contemplate the great eloquence of my previous remarks."[21]

On election day, an impressive 13.4 percent (341,226) of the New York electorate voted for Bill Buckley. John

Lindsay eked out a narrow win, receiving 45.3 percent to Abe Beame's 41.3 percent. Conservatives had denied the *New York Times* the opportunity to proclaim, "Lindsay's decisive victory today catapulted him into a position of national leadership in the Republican Party and established him as a leading presidential possibility in 1968."

The Buckley campaign so energized the Conservative Party of New York that five years later it elected Bill's brother Jim to the U.S. Senate. (Bill Buckley was first approached to make the race but declined.) Buckley's mayoral effort also sketched the outlines of a winning coalition of ethnic, Catholic Democrats and middle-class Republicans. In his landmark study *The Emerging Republican Majority,* Kevin Phillips cited Buckley's vote as a "harbinger" of the new majority. Buckley's 1965 coalition, writes John Judis, "perfectly anticipated" the northern urban coalition that Ronald Reagan forged in 1980 and 1984, which enabled the California conservative to carry New York City in both elections.[22]

But Buckley offered a more pessimistic appraisal of the future, writing in *The Unmaking of a Mayor* that the conservative doctrine lacked "mass appeal." Conservatism in America, he wrote, was a "force" rather than "a political movement." He went so far as to declare that the Republican Party would not survive as "a major party," a probability he deeply regretted, for the alternative was likely to be "a congeries of third parties, adamantly doctrinaire, inadequately led, insufficiently thoughtful, improvidently angry, self-defeatingly sectarian."[23]

Buckley's lamentation was ill-timed. Even as he tore at his garments, a new political star was rising in the West, the Conservative Party of New York was girding for battle, and a new mode of political fundraising (direct mail) was being crafted by Richard Viguerie and others that would enable conservatives to challenge Big Government in Washington, D.C., and various state capitals.

Another outcome of the Buckley campaign was the award-winning *Firing Line*. Buckley and the multitalented Neal Freeman (who had managed the mayoral campaign) had been talking for a year about a television program featuring Buckley versus any and all champions of the Left. Little serious interest was expressed by media executives until the Buckley-Lindsay-Beame debates, and then they came calling. *Firing Line* debuted in April 1966, and would stay on the air for more than thirty-three years.

Television had never seen anything like it: Buckley verbally slicing and dicing liberal opponents like perennial Socialist presidential candidate Norman Thomas, anti–Vietnam War activist Staughton Lynd, TV moderator David Susskind (whom Buckley introduced by saying, "If there were a contest for the title of Mr. Eleanor Roosevelt, he would unquestionably win it"), LSD apostle Timothy Leary, and Beat poet Allen Ginsberg, playing his little harmonium and offering his Hare Krishna chant.[24]

Not everyone was interested in matching wits and words with Buckley. Eager to have Senator Robert F. Kennedy as a guest, the *Firing Line* host offered the late president's brother an honorarium of $500 and a role in determining the format. Kennedy declined. Asked why he thought the New York senator had turned him down, Buckley replied, "Why does baloney reject the grinder?"[25]

Out of the 1,500 programs and the several thousand

guests during the three decades of *Firing Line,* three central themes emerged: Communism, capitalism, and faith—the themes that mattered most to Buckley throughout his life. The reality of Communism came up again and again. British historian Paul Johnson insisted that the nature of twentieth-century totalitarianism, particularly the Soviet variety, was unique and that conventional historical analysis did not tell you how to deal with Soviet aggression. Buckley heartily agreed. Russian dissident Vladimir Bukovsky, "treated" in Soviet mental hospitals for a decade, described how potential opposition in the Soviet Union was suppressed. Buckley was appalled. Henry Kissinger, the master of realpolitik, discussed the inherent dangers in any unequal strategic strength between the Soviets and the United States. Jeane Kirkpatrick, recently returned from Nicaragua, acknowledged that for the first time she saw the possible "disestablishment" of the Marxist state there—which turned out to be the case in the democratic elections of 1990 made possible by the Reagan Doctrine.[26]

Likewise, Buckley debated economics on *Firing Line.* Liberal economist John Kenneth Galbraith—a frequent guest who held his own with his host and friend—stated that he loved taxation because he believed in leveling, regardless of the consequences (or more precisely, because of the consequences). Free marketer George Gilder argued that the risk element of capitalism was what made it a philanthropic social arrangement. Presidential candidate Ronald Reagan endorsed tax cuts across the board and the Laffer curve, to Buckley's delight.[27]

For all his pessimism—and even on a good day, Buckley could be quite pessimistic—he retained his belief that

God knew what he was doing and in any case we should be more concerned about where we end up in the City of God than in the City of Man. He liked to quote the Russian poet Ilya Ehrenburg, who, although a Soviet apologist much of his life, rose to the defense of another Russian poet, Boris Pasternak, with these memorable lines: "If the whole world were to be covered with asphalt, one day a crack would appear in the asphalt; and in that crack grass would grow."[28]

With *Firing Line* guests such as Clare Boothe Luce, former British prime minister Harold Macmillan, philosopher Mortimer Adler, and especially Malcolm Muggeridge, Buckley delved deeply into religion and its place in the modern world. Asked why Whittaker Chambers had written that the Christian church represented the only truly conservative force in the world, Luce replied that the church had preserved for two thousand years a "true view of the nature of man: a creature who is capable of being a saint and who is most of the time a sinner."[29]

When Macmillan, at age eighty-six, was asked about the prospects for the survival of the West, the elder statesman replied that he couldn't understand why so many people who believed so firmly in the brotherhood of man had so much difficulty believing in the fatherhood of God. Paul Johnson spoke to the political consequences of idealism and atheism, saying that in his book *Modern Times* he pointed out that "when you drive toward a utopian state, there is no point of balance; there is no stasis there. . . . You have to drive onwards or else you go backward—and relapse into capitalism. You have to drive onward . . . until you create boat people, and put men like Vladimir Bukovsky in psychiatric asylums."[30]

In their conversation, broadcast at Christmastime, Muggeridge and Buckley agreed that Christendom was probably coming to an end. But there was good news, Muggeridge insisted, quoting St. Augustine on the sacking of Carthage by the barbarians: "This is grievous news, but let us remember if it's happened, then God has willed it; and that men build cities and men destroy cities; that there's also the City of God, and that's where we belong."

"To me," Muggeridge said, "that's the perfect expression." He added, "It's only insofar as we're citizens of the City of God that we can be Christians in the City of Man."

"That we can bear it," responded Buckley.

"That we can bear it," Muggeridge agreed.[31]

This is not an axiom certain to find favor among liberals, but it resonates among conservatives like Bill Buckley, who as a schoolboy in England began all his essays with the initials A.M.D.G.—*Ad Majorem Dei Gloriam* (for the greater glory of God).

Expanding Buckley's popular appeal at this time was *The Unmaking of a Mayor*, which, in the words of liberal biographer Judis, displayed "a stylistic brilliance and a skill in narrative" that far exceeded his early writing. The Buckley of *God and Man at Yale* had "charmed older conservatives and inspired younger ones." The Buckley of *The Unmaking of a Mayor* attracted a far broader range of readers and made Bill Buckley a popular bestselling writer.[32] And the novels were yet to come.

A VERY BAD YEAR

The year 1968 may have been "the most turbulent in American history," writes Jeffrey Hart. Americans were shaken by events ranging from the unexpected Communist offensive of Tet to the assassinations of Martin Luther King and Robert Kennedy to the near anarchy of the Democratic National Convention. Like China, America was experiencing a Great Cultural Revolution with the attempted elimination of the Four Olds—old customs, old habits, old culture, old thinking. Nothing seemed safe or sacred.[33] While the center wavered, conservatives challenged the Left and helped give voice to a Silent Majority. One voice above all others could be heard on the Right—that of William F. Buckley Jr.

Following Tet, Buckley called for the use of nuclear weapons in Vietnam as a way to bring the war to a swift end, a radical course of action that even Barry Goldwater, the alleged wild-eyed bomb-thrower, had never suggested. He described New York City antiwar marchers as "young slobs strutting their epicene resentment." He opposed Pope John XXIII's and Pope Paul VI's support of détente, and he denounced American Catholics, like the Berrigan brothers, who opposed the Vietnam War.[34] He firmly condemned the murders of America's leaders, writing: "[Nothing] in the whole exclamatory spring—not the war, not a Presidential race—shocks the sensibilities so stunningly as Martin Luther King's death in Tennessee. . . . A breathtaking ugliness, coiled like a clock spring, gathered itself and struck."[35]

No one was immune to the ugly mood of the nation, including the usually unflappable Bill Buckley, who lost his temper at the Democratic convention in full view of a national television audience. He and the serpentine Gore Vidal had debated nightly at the Republican National Convention and now at the Democratic meeting, their language becoming more personal and vitriolic at each encounter. On one occasion, the calculatedly provocative Vidal remarked that Buckley would win a contest for "Mr. Myra Breckinridge"—a reference to the transgender "hero" of Vidal's not-so-soft-pornographic novel *Myra Breckinridge*.

In Chicago, Vidal began their conversation by saying, "As far as I am concerned, the only sort of pro- or crypto-Nazi that I can think of is yourself." Which prompted Buckley to angrily respond, "Now listen, you queer, stop calling me a crypto-Nazi or I'll sock you in the goddamn face and you'll stay plastered."[36]

As Bridges and Coyne point out, Buckley was so upset by the explosive exchange that he wrote a 15,000-word article about it in *Esquire* including a semi-apology for calling Vidal a "queer." The magazine published a response by Vidal, who implied, among other things, that Buckley was a homosexual and an anti-Semite. Although urged by friends not to take action, Buckley sued *Esquire* and Vidal for libel. Vidal countersued. Some four years later, *Esquire* settled out of court but publicly apologized to Buckley and reimbursed him for legal expenses.[37]

For Buckley, the 1968 presidential campaign came down to a practical question: who was the most viable conservative candidate? An inviting choice was Barry Goldwater, whose prediction that Vietnam would become an unwinnable war under Johnson's leadership had been vindicated. But Goldwater had already endorsed Richard

Nixon. Another possibility was Ronald Reagan, but he had been governor of California for little more than a year when the campaign began.

That left Nixon. Buckley admired Nixon as the man who had defended Whittaker Chambers against Alger Hiss, but recognized that the former vice president tilted to the left on most domestic issues. And so *National Review*, with James Burnham as author, endorsed Nixon as a "competent, intelligent, experienced, professional politician" known for his "election-machine style of politics." Jeffrey Hart calls the editorial "a fine exposition" of "skeptical conservatism going back to the Constitution and the *Federalist Papers*."[38] It was also a case of hoping for the best and expecting less.

As John Judis points out, Buckley had come a long way from 1955 and his search for the ideal conservative candidate.[39] He was now willing to support an anti-Communist nonconservative who was open to conservative ideas and influence. *NR*'s endorsement was a sharp break even from 1960, when the magazine, stating that it did not engage in practical politics, had declined to state its presidential preference. Here again can be seen the influence of the prudential politics advocated by Burnham and Chambers.

The Nixon endorsement had not just happened: Nixon had wooed Buckley and his colleagues for years, instructing aide Patrick J. Buchanan to talk insider politics with publisher Bill Rusher and personally discussing realpolitik in all its ramifications with Buckley and Burnham. Nixon denied emphatically that he had ever said (as reported by columnist Robert Novak) that "the Buckleyites are a greater menace to the Republican Party than the Birchers."[40]

When Nixon narrowly defeated Hubert Humphrey in November 1968, Buckley and his colleagues took satisfaction, knowing that in the absence of their endorsement the outcome might well have been different.

The result also might have been different had Buckley not gone out of his way to discredit the third-party candidate, the alleged conservative Alabama governor George Wallace. On *Firing Line* he attacked Wallace from the right on economic policy and from the left on race. Buckley later recalled that his design was to show that Wallace's "hold on conservatism really had to do with his racism." He wrote Nancy Reagan that Wallace was "a dangerous man" and his son, Christopher, that Wallace was "Mr. Evil."[41]

Not the One

In the first six months of the Nixon administration, *National Review* was cautiously complimentary, applauding the appointment of Warren Burger to succeed Earl Warren as chief justice and the announcement of welfare reform and revenue-sharing with the states.

Buckley continued his ascendancy. In 1967 he won a Best Columnist of the Year award. In 1969 *Firing Line* won an Emmy. In September 1970 Buckley achieved iconic cultural status when he was the celebrity guest on the top-ranked TV comedy program, *Laugh-In*.

But President Nixon's lurch to the left, especially in foreign policy, was no laughing matter for Buckley and other conservatives. Henry Kissinger's secret trips to Communist China were revealed, and Nixon announced that he would attend summits in Peking and Moscow. In the summer of 1971, the president unveiled what he called his New Economic Plan (Lenin would have applauded the variation on his New Economic Policy), featuring wage and price controls and a new "flexible" tariff policy. "I am now a Keynesian in economics," Nixon declared, an assertion that could not be ignored by conservatives.

Twelve leaders of the Right, with William F. Buckley Jr. at the top of the list, met in New York City and issued a declaration as "The Manhattan Twelve." Citing the dereliction in military preparedness and the turns toward the Soviet Union and Red China, these conservative leaders announced that they were suspending their "support of the Administration."[42] Buckley's unyielding anti-Communism had again led him to take a strong public stand against an American president. He and *NR* went so far as to back Representative John Ashbrook's principled but impractical run against Nixon in the 1972 New Hampshire Republican primary. Only 10 percent of Republican voters cast their ballots for Ashbrook in the three states in which he ran, but fundamental conservative principles had been articulated—principles like limited government and a firm stand against Communism, which the Nixon administration had abandoned.

To his surprise, Buckley was assigned a seat on the Nixon plane going to China, affording him a rhetorical opportunity of which he took full advantage. Repulsed by the spectacle of an American president greeting and toasting the top Chinese Communist officials at a formal Peking dinner, he wrote these memorable lines: "The effect was as if Sir Hartley Shawcross had suddenly risen from the prosecutor's stand at Nuremberg and descended to embrace Goering and Goebbels and Doenitz and Hess, begging them to join him in the making of a better world."[43]

Buckley was even more startled in the summer of 1973 when the White House invited him to serve as an American delegate to the United Nations, an organization he had used as a piñata from his earliest days. He at first demurred but then accepted, having been promised a place on the UN's Third Committee, which deals with human rights, and because in a spasm of "pure undiluted Walter Mitty-ism" he imagined that any delegate armed with a copy of the Universal Declaration of Human Rights could make the Third Committee his personal forum.[44] He saw himself holding the other delegates spellbound as he read from Solzhenitsyn, described the concentration camps in Communist China, and pleaded the case for this or that incarcerated dissident.

In the end, his every attempt to discuss human rights candidly in the Third Committee was squelched as not being in accord with détente, the official U.S.-Nixon-Kissinger policy. While conceding that one could refer to certain nonideological achievements in areas such as science and health and the usefulness perhaps of the General Assembly as a place where "the little countries can speak their minds," Buckley summed up his UN experience in one sentence: "The United Nations is the most concentrated assault on moral reality in the history of free institutions."[45]

Meanwhile, cracks were appearing in the seemingly smooth Nixon façade. On January 11, 1973, Senate Majority Leader Mike Mansfield (D-MT) announced that Senator Sam Ervin (D-NC) would head an inquiry into

Watergate. Almost from the beginning, *NR* took a strong stand, saying editorially, "This Watergate affair . . . has acquired a sour, rotting quality that can only be cleaned up by the truth. . . . The Administration should purge itself of any person of whatever level whose relation to the Watergate affair was legally or morally culpable."[46] Burnham was the author of the editorial, Buckley having recused himself from commenting in the magazine because of his longtime friendship with Howard Hunt, organizer of the break-in.

In the ensuing nineteen months, Nixon dodged and ducked, insisting to conservatives like Senator Barry Goldwater that he had no knowledge of Watergate, reluctantly accepting the resignations of his top aides H. R. Haldeman and John Ehrlichman, firing various attorneys general (Richard Kleindienst and Elliot Richardson), and clinging stubbornly to the mast of the White House. At long last, on August 9, 1974, Richard M. Nixon resigned as president rather than face certain impeachment by the House of Representatives and probable conviction by the Senate for obstruction of justice, abuse of power, and contempt of Congress.

Buckley believed that Nixon had brought his troubles down on himself. He wrote in his column that the president "had teased the Puritan conscience of America and loosed the hounds that finally arrived at his door." As with the Goldwater candidacy a decade earlier, Buckley was concerned about the deleterious impact of Nixon's exit on the conservative movement.[47]

As early as October 1973, he had written to Reagan, then in his next to last year as governor of California, that "Our Leader [their code name for Nixon] is in deep trouble, and that it is altogether possible that he will not succeed, finally, in extricating himself." The following July, shortly before it was revealed that Nixon had been aware of the Watergate cover-up—the so-called smoking gun—Buckley warned Reagan, "Don't make the mistake of hanging in there too long."[48] Reagan did not heed Buckley's advice, being one of the very last Republicans to call for Nixon's resignation. "I have just a sneaking instinct," he wrote Buckley, "that there may have been, with regard to our leader, overkill."[49]

Buckley had already been obliged to put into perspective the ignominious departure of Vice President Spiro Agnew—a national conservative hero—who had resigned his office after pleading *nolo contendere* to a charge of income tax evasion. Agnew privately admitted to Goldwater, among others, that as governor of Maryland he had accepted political contributions totaling tens of thousands of dollars from people who did business with the state. He continued to receive money from them as vice president, pocketing envelopes thick with cash during meetings in his White House office.[50]

At the annual dinner of the Conservative Party of New York, Buckley stressed that conservatives should not make the mistake of defending Agnew as liberals had defended Alger Hiss in the 1950s. Rather, they should separate the "valid ideas" Agnew had espoused from the misconduct of the man. *Human Events* was less diplomatic, saying the vice president had "traded away" his many attributes— including giving voice to the Silent Majority—"for a mess of pottage."[51]

First Agnew's resignation in disgrace, then Nixon's

forced departure to avoid impeachment. What next? President Gerald Ford provided the answer: the nomination of ultraliberal New York governor Nelson Rockefeller as his vice president.

Many conservatives favored the man they still thought of as "Mr. Conservative," Senator Barry Goldwater, although others preferred Ronald Reagan. Instead, Ford named the man whose malicious misrepresentations of Goldwater during the 1964 Republican primaries had been used by Democrats to bury the senator in the general election.

Some tough-minded young conservatives were mad as hell and unwilling to take it anymore. Led by direct-mail guru Richard Viguerie, they formed an informal group of political activists and Capitol Hill aides that became the New Right. They were, in the words of author and columnist Kevin Phillips, "anti-establishment, middle-class political rebels more interested in issues like abortion, gun control, busing, ERA, quotas, bureaucracy, and the grassroots tax revolt than in capital gains taxation or natural gas deregulation."[52] They were also firmly anti-Communist, providing a link to the conservatives grouped around *National Review* and Bill Buckley.

But there were disconnects between New Right leaders and Buckley, starting with Viguerie's enthusiasm for George Wallace. The Texas-born Viguerie insisted that he and Alabama's Democratic governor agreed on about "80 percent of the important issues, social issues like busing and law and order, and the need for a strong national defense."[53] In his eagerness to forge an alliance between Republican economic conservatives and Democratic social conservatives, Viguerie was willing to downplay and even overlook Wallace's earlier and adamant stand against civil rights for African Americans, as well as his fondness for government solutions to public problems.

Buckley was skeptical about the New Right's attempt to fuse populism and conservatism in the person of Wallace. Taking up the issue of higher energy costs, for example, Buckley argued that a conservative would pass along higher costs to the consumer in order to encourage more exploration, but a populist would seek a villain like the big oil companies. "That's the kind of thing that rolls off George Wallace's tongue naturally," he wrote.[54]

Kevin Phillips, who coined the phrase "The New Right" and endorsed most of the New Right's policy positions, launched a series of highly personal attacks on Bill Buckley. He criticized Buckley for joining the establishment Council on Foreign Relations and "abandoning Middle America to load up his yacht with vintage wines and sail across the Atlantic." He faulted *National Review* for lauding conservative intellectuals Wilhelm Röpke and Eric Voegelin, asking sarcastically, "So what have they to say to Kansas City and Scranton?"[55]

In his syndicated column, *NR* senior editor Jeffrey Hart responded that *National Review* was never intended to be a mass circulation magazine. Its founders assumed that in Middle America, "and yes in Kansas City and Scranton," there resided individuals "addicted to good prose and to theoretical perception" who possessed "unprecedented leverage." *NR*'s founders, Hart wrote, saw that conservatism must be viable "as an intellectual as well as a popular and political presence."[56]

An adamant Phillips remained dismissive of Buckley and the other "elitists" at *National Review*. A more gracious note was struck by Richard Viguerie, who, in his bestselling manifesto *The New Right: We're Ready to Lead*, wrote that it was Buckley's "unique contribution" to draw together three kinds of conservatives in America—classical liberals like Frank Chodorov, traditional conservatives like Russell Kirk, and anti-Communists like Whittaker Chambers. "The New Right owes much of what we believe in and are fighting for," Viguerie said, "to such outstanding men and the catalyst who brought them together, William F. Buckley Jr."[57]

There were now four kinds of conservatives: classical liberals or libertarians, traditional conservatives, anti-Communists, and New Right populists or social conservatives. A fifth variety would soon appear, the neoconservatives, with whom Buckley, the master fusionist, would form a close relationship.

MUGGED BY REALITY

A series of events in the late 1960s and early 1970s jolted a small but influential group of old-fashioned liberals—mostly Jewish and residing in New York City—and forced them to move out of their no longer comfortable Democratic digs. The happenings included the 1972 presidential nomination of ultraliberal George McGovern; the seeming willingness of modern liberals to let Vietnam and any other nation under siege fall into the hands of the Communists; the refusal of prominent Democrats to fault the United Nations for its virulent anti-Israel rhetoric; and the revolution in sexual and social relations that produced what the liberal critic Lionel Trilling called the "adversary culture."

In Irving Kristol's memorable phrase, neoconservatives were liberals who had been "mugged by reality." They attacked the radicals as despoilers of the liberal tradition. Kristol called for a return to the "republican virtue" of the founding fathers and invoked the idea of a good society. He endorsed the notion of a "moral and political order" and conceded that the idea of a "hidden hand" had its uses in the marketplace.[58] Confronted with reality, the founder of neoconservatism did not merely endorse but embraced conservative principles and practices.

Mainstream conservatives warmly welcomed Kristol and his friends. Buckley set the tone by declaring that Kristol was "writing more sense in the public interest these days than anybody I can think of." The two men had gotten to know each other at a monthly luncheon group called the Boys Club, organized by Buckley and the New York liberal intellectual Richard Clurman. Harvard social scientists Daniel Patrick Moynihan and Nathan Glazer noticed they were being treated in *National Review* "with a much higher level of intellectual honesty" than in liberal journals.[59] Buckley recognized the formidable brain power of the neoconservatives and their ready access to the mass media, attributes which would serve the conservative movement well.

In the early 1970s, as *NR* approached its twentieth anniversary, there were grumblings that its editor-in-chief had become so great a celebrity that he was growing indifferent to the course of the magazine and the conservative movement he had founded—charges that had little merit when one considers his frenetic schedule of TV programs, newspaper columns, lectures, and editorial involvement in *National Review*. It was at this moment that Buckley published an intriguing and too-little-known work, *Four Reforms: A Guide for the Seventies.*

In just 128 pages, the author proposes solutions for four of the most persistent problems in modern America—welfare, taxes, education, and crime. Regarding welfare, he first suggests that "the burden of the nonprofessional work done on behalf of the aged" be done by high school graduates who would voluntarily donate one year of service before going on to college. He then proposes a series of governmental reforms including the appropriation of federal funds for social welfare only to states whose per capita income "is below the national average."[60] In his *New York Times* book review, Daniel Patrick Moynihan, then ambassador to India and later a safely liberal U.S. senator from New York, rejected Buckley's welfare reform, saying that the people who needed welfare were "as likely to be found in high income states as in low." But Moynihan offered no alternative, contenting himself with saying, erroneously, that the problem "will have greatly receded by the mid-1980s."[61] In fact, the "problem" receded only in 1996 when a Republican Congress passed historic welfare reform over President Bill Clinton's veto—twice.

With regard to taxes, Buckley reflects the influence of Albert Jay Nock and Milton Friedman by proposing the elimination of the progressive income tax and the institution of a flat tax of 15 percent on all income.

Taking up education, he suggests a constitutional amendment incorporating the Supreme Court's *Brown v. Board of Education* decision and forbidding the denial of "any relief authorized by any legislature for children attending non-public schools." (Catholics and evangelicals heartily endorsed this reform.) As Moynihan said, the treatment of Catholic schools was "a scandal of American juridical and political liberalism."[62] Perhaps in due course, Buckley writes, "we shall move into a voucher system . . . at any grade school." Until that day, "the immediate concern is to husband such private schools as there are."[63]

He concludes with the hardest of lines on crime, proposing that the Fifth Amendment be repealed and procedures regarding an accused person should adhere to the criterion: "Did he do it?" He adds that the goal should be "speedier justice."[64]

Commenting on an earlier Buckley book, *Cruising Speed,* the *Christian Science Monitor* said that Bill Buckley's writing "forces the reader to give up or think."[65] Buckley liked that judgment so much he reprinted it on the inside back cover of *Four Reforms.*

Even the protean Buckley did not accomplish all these things all by himself. Longtime associate Linda Bridges has estimated that at the long height of his career (from 1966 to 1999), he kept busy a secretary, one and sometimes two typists, and four researchers. (The researchers he shared with the magazine.) This supporting group did not include the *NR* staff, the *Firing Line* production staff, and a limousine and driver that enabled him to work—dictating a letter, polishing an essay or a speech—while going from place to place.[66]

One of Bill Buckley's most significant public-policy contributions to the modern conservative movement (and to the Reagan presidency) was as an early champion of supply-side economics. As the historian Brian Domitrovic points out, among participants in public debate, Buckley was "the *one* who spotted nascent supply-side economics" in early 1971. A concrete Buckley action was to hire a young economist, Alan Reynolds, making *NR* the first journal of public opinion to have a writer with a supply-side perspective on staff.

National Review, Domitrovic says, "was the lone beacon" (even before the *Wall Street Journal*) "pointing the way out of a nearly unprecedented economic darkness in the early 1970s." The solution: stable money and tax cuts, major elements of what came to be called the supply-side revolution. Buckley also used *Firing Line* to deflate old Keynesians like John Kenneth Galbraith and raise up supply-siders like George Gilder, Arthur Laffer, and Robert Bartley. He later remarked, with obvious satisfaction: "It is not wide of the historical mark to say that during the years *Firing Line* has been produced, socialism has collapsed."[67]

SAILING AND SAVING

As he approached fifty, Bill Buckley resolved to sail across the Atlantic Ocean in his sailboat *Cyrano,* a long-held dream. He also responded positively to an intriguing suggestion from his book editor Samuel Vaughan to write a novel.

Buckley's authorial model was the popular spy novelist Frederick Forsyth, who had written *The Day of the*

Jackal and *The Odessa File*—not John le Carré, an apostle of moral and political equivalence. Buckley later explained that he had "only a single idea in mind. . . . I would write a book in which the good guys and the bad guys were actually distinguishable from one another. I took a deep breath and further resolved that the good guys would be—the Americans."[68]

To correct the record about the CIA—which he insisted "seeks to advance the honorable alternative in the struggle for the world"—he created the character of CIA operative Blackford Oakes, who was young, dashing, "distinctively American." Buckley's first novel, *Saving the Queen,* was greeted by generally favorable reviews and quickly achieved bestseller status. Buckley's favorite review was reportedly the one by a liberal professor of English at the University of Missouri, who confessed he liked the novel but salved his conscience by adding, "The hero of *Saving the Queen* . . . is tall, handsome, witty, agreeable, compassionate and likeable, from which at least we can take comfort in knowing that the book is not autobiographical."[69] As readers of this work know, the similarities between Oakes and Buckley are in fact numerous.

The second Blackford Oakes novel, *Stained Glass,* published in 1978, won the American Book Award as the best suspense novel of the year. There would follow nine more Oakes novels, culminating in *Last Call for Blackford Oakes,* which appeared in 2005. Each book demonstrated that the CIA and the KGB were not the mirror image of each other any more than the United States and the Soviet Union were.

Buckley's favorite mode of relaxation—even in gale force winds—was sailing. He had learned to sail as a child on a lake in northwestern Connecticut and kept a succession of boats at Wallacks Point, on the Connecticut shore of Long Island Sound. His son, Christopher, wrote that his father's greatness "was of a piece with the way he conducted himself at sea." Great men, he said, "always have too much sail up." They take great risks and they are ever impatient—for the next adventure.[70]

In 1975, Bill Buckley, Christopher, and the rest of the crew sailed across the Atlantic, starting in Miami and four thousand miles later dropping anchor in the shadow of Gibraltar. They had such a good time that Bill Buckley declared they must sail across the Pacific, which they did, from Honolulu to New Guinea, ten years later. As they made their way across the endless Pacific, Christopher Buckley felt more and more like Christopher Columbus searching eagerly for land, for an island where they could swim without someone standing "shark-guard" with an assault rifle, and for a stretch of sleep longer than four hours.[71]

The moment they dropped anchor, Bill Buckley would look at this watch and say, "Okay, it's ten o'clock now. What say we shove off at two?" Christopher was learning that for his father "it was the voyage, not the stopping. Great men are not idlers. . . . They're built for speed."[72]

CHAPTER 4

THE BUILDER

Wherever he was—in New Guinea, Gstaad, or Wallacks Point—Bill Buckley kept his eye on the state of the conservative movement, including and most especially the political fortunes of Ronald Reagan. The two conservatives had first met in January 1961 when Reagan, then the host of the popular television program *GE Theater,* was to introduce Buckley to an assembly of mostly doctors and their wives at a Los Angeles high school. However, it was discovered that the microphone was dead, and the control room at the rear of the hall was locked. As the audience grew increasingly restive at the delay of the program, Reagan decided to take remedial action.

The future president walked to the side of the hall and looked through the window at the ledge running the length of the building some two stories above traffic. He slipped out the window and with his back to the wall sidestepped carefully on the parapet toward the control-room

129

window. Reaching it, he broke the glass with his elbow and disappeared into the control room. "In a minute there was light in the upstairs room," Buckley later wrote, "and then we could hear the crackling of the newly animated microphone."[1]

For Buckley, Reagan's movements that night were a "nifty allegory of his approach to foreign policy"—the calm appraisal of a situation, the willingness to take risks, and then the decisive moment "leading to lights and sound—and music, the music of the spheres."[2]

The Yale University graduate and the Eureka College alumnus had much in common: Each was tall (Reagan 6′1″, Buckley 6′2″), handsome, ambitious, a gifted speaker with a ready wit, an inveterate reader with an abiding interest in ideas, and a star in his profession. Each was a committed conservative—Reagan the zealous convert from liberalism, Buckley the cradle conservative. Each had a strong libertarian streak and viewed government almost always as the problem, not the solution. Each was a fierce anti-Communist who believed that you could only trust the Communists to be Communists—although Reagan would come to believe that you could trust some Communists if you carefully verified their actions. A close friendship developed, reinforced by Nancy Reagan's warm approval of Bill and Pat Buckley, who knew many of the same socially prominent New Yorkers she did.

There was a significant intellectual difference between the two conservatives: Buckley's innate skepticism—deepened by the influence of Whittaker Chambers and James Burnham—about the possibility of altering the course of history contrasted with Reagan's sunny belief that, in the words of Thomas Paine, "We have it in our power to begin the world over again."[3]

When Reagan ran for governor of California in 1966, *NR* enthusiastically endorsed his candidacy. By the early 1970s, Buckley was convinced that "Reagan was capable of becoming President."[4] Following Agnew's exit in disgrace in 1973, the magazine dubbed Reagan the leader of conservatism. But after twenty often frustrating years of building a conservative alternative to the liberal establishment, Buckley could not help wondering what there was to lead.

In a November 1975 interview, a saturnine Buckley said: "As of this moment [the movement] is going nowhere." At the twentieth-anniversary dinner of *National Review*, Buckley described in detail the leftward tilt of Western civilization, led by American capitalists "fleeing into the protective arms of the government at the least hint of commercial difficulty." He suggested that survival might well depend upon something like Albert Jay Nock's Remnant.

Still, he would not submit to despair, because from the right angle it could be seen that "Communism is theoretically and empirically discredited." All over the world, he said, "enslaved people continue to dream about freedom." Inroads against poverty were successful "in almost exact correspondence to the vitality of the private sector." And most significant of all, "there are no signs at all that God is dead. He appears to have survived even Vatican II."[5]

In these remarks we see the three major ideas that guided Bill Buckley from the beginning of his career: a contempt for Communism, a firm belief in private enterprise, and an abiding faith in God. As at previous anniversary dinners, Buckley pledged that he and the magazine would continue to persevere. "We have stood together for one-tenth the life span of this Republic," he said, "and we must resolve to stand with it, and its ideals, forever."[6]

In the same interview in which Buckley said that the conservative movement was "going nowhere," he added, "That would change if Reagan were to decide to challenge Mr. Ford in the primary." Some conservatives, including leaders of the New Right and *NR* publisher William Rusher (but not Buckley), were pushing the idea of starting a third, conservative party. Reagan disavowed any interest in the idea. Conservatives lustily cheered Reagan at the 1975 meeting of the Conservative Political Action Conference (CPAC) when he asked, "Is it a third party that we need, or is it a new and revitalized second party, raising a banner of no pale pastels, but bold colors which make it unmistakably clear where we stand on all the issues troubling the people?"[7]

Reagan hesitated and then decided to do as Buckley had suggested: challenge incumbent president Gerald Ford for the 1976 Republican presidential nomination. A turning point for Reagan had been Ford's refusal to meet with famed Russian dissident and author Aleksandr Solzhenitsyn. For Reagan and Buckley there was no greater anti-Communist than the man who wrote *One Day in the Life of Ivan Denisovich* and *The Gulag Archipelago*. "The public acclaim by Solzhenitsyn of the kind of thing we were doing," Buckley said, "was an enormous stroke in the ideological heavens and his Gulag book simply broke the back of the intellectual pro-Communist left."[8]

Buckley shared the movement's elation when Reagan sought his party's nomination—he had been encouraging Reagan to seek the presidency since at least 1973, and backed his bid in his column, although he played no formal role in the campaign. He felt sharp disappointment when Ford won the nomination in a heartbreakingly close vote at the national convention—1,187 delegates to 1,070. Reagan thanked his advisers and workers, many of whom were weeping, and reminded them that although "we lost . . . the cause goes on." And he added a couple of lines from an old Scottish ballad, "I'll lay me down and bleed awhile; though I am wounded, I am not slain. I shall rise and fight again."[9]

Although James Burnham suggested Jimmy Carter as worthy of *NR*'s support (Burnham pointed to Carter's exemplary naval service and his farming background), Buckley stuck with Gerald Ford, who, he said, "had adopted the Reagan line" and accepted the Republican Party platform, drafted by two staunch Reaganites—Senator Jesse Helms of North Carolina and Representative Jack Kemp of New York. When, in a presidential debate, Ford declared, "There is no Soviet domination of Eastern Europe," Buckley attempted but failed to explain away one of the most indefensible assertions in modern politics. President Ford's statement that "I don't believe that the Poles consider themselves dominated by the Soviet Union" was "the ultimate Polish joke," said Buckley.[10] Most Americans did not get the joke and elected Carter president.

They soon regretted their vote. By mid-1979 the inflation rate stood at 13.3 percent, unemployment was 8 percent, and the economy had stalled. Instead of acknowledging his own ineptitude, the ever-sanctimonious Carter faulted the American people, who, he said, were deep in the throes of a "crisis of confidence." The president was unwilling to concede that Americans were being strangled by "stagflation" (zero economic growth coupled with double-digit inflation), a condition created by the Carter administration.[11]

To the Rescue

Ronald Reagan was very nearly the perfect conservative candidate—charismatic, articulate, experienced, and principled. In January 1978, two years before the presidential campaign was expected to begin, Bill Buckley in his syndicated column effectively endorsed the sixty-six-year-old Ronald Reagan for president. He directly addressed the question of whether the former California governor was too old by recounting how Reagan had insisted on participating in a touch football game the preceding Thanksgiving at the Buckley estate and was "indistinguishable" in his energy and skills from his eighteen-year-old son, Ron Jr. Buckley predicted that voters, if asked whether Reagan should run, would reply, after noting Reagan's obvious energy and fitness, "Why not?"[12]

A decisive turn to the right in politics seemed possible—and not only in America. In May 1979, the Conservative Party won control of the British Parliament, and Margaret Thatcher became the new prime minister. In a euphoric column titled "Margaret Is My Darling," Buckley pointed out that Thatcher had a large mess to clean up but concluded: "Evelyn Waugh complained that the trouble with our century is that we never succeeded in turning the clock back a single second. The voters may now have proved him wrong."[13] Thatcher and Reagan would become close political allies who, together with Pope John Paul II, would institute the strategic and other policies that brought the forty-year-old Cold War to a peaceful and unexpectedly swift end.

Declaring his candidacy in November 1979, Reagan went on to best six of the GOP's brightest in the presidential primaries: Senate Republican leader Howard Baker; former treasury secretary John Connally; Senator Bob Dole, the 1976 vice presidential nominee; Congressman Phil Crane, chairman of the American Conservative Union; liberal congressman John Anderson; and George H. W. Bush, former everything, including U.S. envoy to China, CIA director, and chairman of the Republican National Committee.

Buckley and Reagan saw each other during the 1980 campaign and frequently talked on the telephone, but rarely discussed political strategy. One exception: when Reagan fired campaign manager John Sears just before the New Hampshire primary and replaced him with Bill Casey, he called Buckley to ask for his support. One lasting Buckley contribution was his strong recommendation that the Reagan campaign hire the Pulitzer Prize–winning reporter Tony Dolan—a Yale graduate—as a speechwriter. Dolan went on to become a key speechwriter during the eight White House years. "The best thing Buckley did," said Casey later, "was bugging me into hiring a guy named Tony Dolan."[14]

Before and after Reagan was nominated, Buckley delighted in squelching insinuations about the former actor's mental capacity. He wrote, for example, that Reagan was "simple minded enough to cherish no other ideals than those of the Founding Fathers." After the national Republican convention, Buckley acted as an intermediary between Reagan and his old friend Henry Kissinger, who was in touch with wives of the American hostages in Iran. The former secretary of state had secured the willingness of their spokeswoman to issue a "contradictory statement" if President Carter should denounce Reagan's stand on the hostages. Buckley also told Reagan, with tongue in cheek, that Kissinger "would be willing to make a public declaration of his non-availability for public office."[15]

In the same playful manner, Buckley wrote Reagan that he thought he would be elected but assured the future president and longtime friend that he aspired to no government job of any kind. Reagan immediately wrote back that he was disappointed. "I had in mind," he informed Buckley, "to appoint you ambassador to Afghanistan"—which the Soviets had invaded the preceding winter, precipitating a prolonged and bloody conflict. Buckley responded in kind that he would accept the challenging assignment. For the next eight years, in many of his communications with President Reagan, he would report on his "secret mission" to Kabul, "where, in our fiction, I lived and worked." In his letters to Buckley, President Reagan sometimes addressed him as "Mr. Ambassador."[16]

As election day approached, conservatives reflected on the lessons learned in the past decades as, led by Bill Buckley, they had built their movement:

- It is not enough to be philosophically right, political strategist Morton Blackwell was fond of saying. You must also be technologically proficient. Conservatives

must be expert in such tools of politics as precinct organization, communications, canvassing, direct mail,
and polling.

- Conservatives must work together. There is not only
safety but also strength in numbers.

- Conservatives should be realistic in their goals and
patient about their realization. Like the Fabians in
Great Britain and the progressives in America, conservatives must prepare themselves for a long march.

- Conservatives should be prudently optimistic, trust-
ing in the ultimate good sense of the American people
to make the right political decisions if given the right
information.

From the founding of *National Review,* Bill Buckley had worked to implement such ideas. He had been no
armchair intellectual; he had engaged in direct political
action, as with the founding of Young Americans for Freedom and the Conservative Party of New York, and running for mayor of New York City. He had labored hard
and successfully to bring together conservatives of varying backgrounds and beliefs. Influenced by Burnham and
Chambers, he had generally adopted a pragmatic attitude
regarding political goals.

His ingrained pessimism, however, had blunted any
deep confidence in the ability of the people—the masses—
to make the right decisions, with or without the necessary
information. And yet he understood full well the many
flaws of the elite, accounting for his early witticism, "I

should sooner live in a society governed by the first two thousand names in the Boston telephone directory than in a society governed by the two thousand faculty members of Harvard University."[17] The putdown of the Harvard faculty is consistent with his criticism of the self-absorbed Yale faculty in *God and Man at Yale* and suggests a willingness to be persuaded, at certain times, of the wisdom of the masses.

Although most of the national polls reported that the 1980 presidential election would be close, Reagan won in an electoral landslide and by more than eight million popular votes. He carried forty-four states (the same number as Lyndon Johnson in his runaway victory over Barry Goldwater in 1964), with a total of 489 electoral votes. His total of 43.9 million votes was the second largest on record, behind only Nixon's 47.2 million in 1972. This conservative triumph provided solid evidence about the aptitude of "We the people" to govern—as would the political triumphs that followed, from Reagan to Newt Gingrich to the early George W. Bush, and the bright constellation of conservative philosophers, popularizers, and politicians who emerged in the coming years.

Reagan's political coattails helped the GOP to pick up twelve seats in the Senate in 1980, giving it majority control for the first time in a quarter of a century. House Republicans gained thirty-three seats, almost all of them conservatives. Former Democratic presidential candidate George McGovern said that the voters had "abandoned American liberalism." The *Washington Post* acknowledged that 1980 was not an ordinary election year: "Nothing of that size and force and sweep," the *Post* editorialized, "could have been created over a weekend or even a week or two by the assorted mullahs and miseries of our times." Liberal pollster Louis Harris concluded that Reagan had won "his stunning victory" because conservatives of all varieties, particularly the Moral Majority, "gave him such massive support."[18]

As he often did, columnist George Will put the victory in perspective and credited the person most responsible (after the candidate himself) for it: "What happened in 1980," he said, "is that American conservatism came of age." Speaking at the twenty-fifth-anniversary dinner of *National Review*, Will noted that sixteen years before, Barry Goldwater had made the Republican Party "a vessel of conservatism" and that *NR* had filled the vessel with "an intellectually defensible modern conservatism." The principal architect of that achievement, he said, was William F. Buckley, "the Pope of the conservative movement, operating out of a little Vatican on 35th Street."[19]

It is a felicitous phrase, but I suggest a different metaphor: William F. Buckley Jr. was the St. Paul of the conservative movement, proselytizing tirelessly across America, fighting the good fight against liberal heretics, exhorting and, when necessary, warning the conservative faithful to mend their ways, knowing the race was not over, even with the coming of the Reagan presidency.

A CONSERVATIVE ESTABLISHMENT

Ronald Reagan came to the presidency with several important political advantages. He had an express mandate from the American people, who knew what he intended to do: cut income taxes from top to bottom, reduce the size of the federal government for the first time since the New Deal, and make the American military number one in the world. To help in this revolutionary task, he had a Republican Senate and a feisty Republican minority in the House determined to avoid legislative gridlock. And he had something else—a vital, committed conservative movement.

Reagan could turn to the Heritage Foundation, the American Enterprise Institute, the Center for Strategic and International Studies, and other think tanks for ideas.

He could call on groups like the American Conservative Union, the National Rifle Association, and the National Right to Life Committee for political muscle.

He could staff his administration with professionals who had gotten their start in the movement, such as Richard V. Allen, Tony Dolan, and Kenneth Cribb.

He could ask neoconservatives like Jeane Kirkpatrick, Kenneth Adelman, and Elliott Abrams for foreign-policy assistance.

He could depend on the support of opinion molders like Bill Buckley, George Will, and Patrick J. Buchanan.

Buckley was proud of his and *National Review*'s decades-old contribution to the Reagan triumph, but he did not hesitate to question the president. From tax cuts to the Strategic Defense Initiative (SDI), Buckley would make his case on issues through *NR*, his column, and his many friends and protégés who populated the administration. The Buckleyites included Aram Bakshian and Tony Dolan in the White House speechwriting office, Christopher Buckley as a speechwriter for Vice President George

H. W. Bush, Daniel Oliver as general counsel to the Department of Education, Evan Galbraith as U.S. ambassador to France, Jim Buckley as undersecretary of state for security assistance, and Bill Casey as director of the CIA.

"Whenever there is a big philosophical issue and people want to weigh in," Casey said, "Buckley can make a call. But he is quite cautious about doing it." Dolan traced Buckley's reticence to his sense of propriety. "You do not disturb a transcendent relationship, that is, a friendship, for the sake of 'I don't like the way the trade bill is going.'" For his part, Reagan would call Buckley or Bill Rusher to discuss a column or an item in *NR*. He was determined not to be cut off from old friends, even if he did not necessarily take their advice.[20]

Buckley and the president conducted a high-spirited correspondence that ranged from Buckley inviting Reagan—after he left office—to take a part in the theatrical version of his spy novel *Stained Glass* to a sharp debate about the treaty eliminating intermediate-range ballistic missiles.

In the first half of 1982, Bill Buckley, the intractable anti-Communist, pressed the Reagan administration to declare war on Cuba because "it is difficult to think of a measure that would give greater heart to the entire anti-communist defense enterprise." He also criticized the president for offering to reopen negotiations on an arms control treaty with the Soviet Union just a few months after he had broken off talks as a protest against the Polish Communist government's suppression of Solidarity. Buckley's faith in Reagan as a champion of freedom was justified by the president's pivotal speech to the National Association of Evangelicals in which he described the

Soviet Union as the "focus of evil in the modern world" and the center of an "evil empire." When a *New York Times* columnist attacked Reagan for using religion to promote a political cause, Buckley retorted, "Mr. Reagan, as leader of the Free World, does well to remind us that we are dealing with men explicitly bound to the proposition that the morality of advancing world revolution is superordinated to any other morality."[21]

As Jeffrey Hart writes, Ronald Reagan set down four goals for his administration: (1) restore the American spirit of confidence and optimism; (2) get the American economy "humming" through cuts in tax rates and domestic spending; (3) build up and "renovate" American military power; and (4) stop the spread of Soviet power and "destroy" the Soviet system through the use of "moral-intellectual and economic-strategic power."[22] *NR* and Buckley endorsed and applauded all four objectives enthusiastically and frequently, although neither the magazine nor its editor appreciated fully that Reagan's deliberate buildup of the American military was calculated to enable him to sit down with the Soviets and negotiate—from strength—the elimination of nuclear weapons and bring about a peaceful end to the Cold War.

Reagan made his foreign-policy intentions clear in four speeches that alerted the Soviets that a new man and a new strategy were in place in Washington, D.C. The new policy was far different from Nixon-Kissinger détente.

Speaking to the British Parliament in June 1982, the president boldly predicted that the "march of freedom and democracy . . . will leave Marxism-Leninism on the ash heap of history." In his talk to the evangelical ministers in March 1983, Reagan presented the moral and religious case for freedom and against tyranny, describing the Soviet Union as "an evil empire." In June 1987, standing in front of the Brandenburg Gate in Berlin, the president delivered perhaps his best-remembered address, declaring, "Mr. Gorbachev, open this gate! Mr. Gorbachev, tear down this wall!" The fourth speech came in May 1988, when Reagan offered an ode to freedom to an audience of mesmerized Russian students at Moscow State University.[23]

Rabidly opposed to Reagan's military buildup were the nuclear freeze and peace movements, whose position Walter Mondale endorsed in the 1984 presidential campaign and the Democrats reiterated in their national platform. *National Review* skillfully skewered the arguments of the freeze movement while emphasizing the involvement of Soviet intelligence within the World Peace Council and the U.S. Peace Council and at New York City's Riverside Church, the favorite meeting place of the peaceniks. *NR* senior editor Joseph Sobran provided an apt metaphor for the intimate relationship—the Hive. "When the Queen Bee in Moscow buzzes, the buzz goes down all through the Hive, buzz, buzz, buzz."[24]

When Mikhail Gorbachev became general secretary of the Soviet Communist Party in 1985, *National Review* wisecracked, "There is room for optimism over the accession to power of Mikhail Gorbachev. He has never been directly linked to the shooting of the Pope."[25] But the magazine, however inadvertently, was acknowledging a critical point—Gorbachev was a different kind of Soviet leader, as Margaret Thatcher and Ronald Reagan realized upon meeting him. In Thatcher's words after her first meeting with Gorbachev, "We can do business together." Reagan prudently added the codicil, "Trust, but verify."[26]

The liberal biographer John Judis, writing in 1988, argues that in the 1980s a general "malaise" afflicted Buckley's writing and affected *National Review* and *Firing Line.* According to Judis, both the magazine and the TV program "appeared detached from national politics and exerted very little influence." But as we have seen, *NR* was very much engaged with the core issues of the day such as nuclear weapons, while *Firing Line* highlighted prominent policy makers and pundits such as Ronald Reagan, Newt Gingrich, George H. W. Bush, Eugene McCarthy, Jesse Helms, Jack Kemp, Jeane Kirkpatrick, Henry Kissinger, the Dalai Lama, Robert Bork, Thomas Sowell, Edward Teller, Phyllis Schlafly, Paul Weyrich, William Rusher, and Malcolm Muggeridge, whose Christmas appearance was rebroadcast several times.

If the man and his rhetoric were less combative than they had been in 1950s and 1960s, it was because the times were different. Buckley was no longer alone in the lists but the spokesman—second only to Ronald Reagan—of a conservative phalanx out to change the direction of the nation and the world. Conservative ideas like winning the Cold War and rolling back the welfare state were no longer derided but widely debated. Communism was not expanding but contracting. Capitalism was spreading from continent to continent, inspiring some conservatives to say, "Now we are all Hayekians." But, cautioned Buckley in an address about F. A. Hayek to the Mont Pelerin Society, "What we do not need is anything that suggests that human freedom is going to lead us to Utopia."[27]

There were many targets of opportunity for a conservative, and Buckley took careful aim at most of them. In May 1983, for example, with purple-hatted bishops of the Catholic Church sitting in the front row, Buckley delivered a lecture at a Catholic college on "moral distinctions and modern warfare." A central proposition of his remarks: "To venerate life is to attach to it first importance. Surely if we were all to do that, any talk of war, just or unjust, prudent or imprudent, limited or unlimited, provoked or unprovoked, would be an exercise in moral atavism."[28]

During a tribute to President Reagan in 1985, on the occasion of *National Review*'s thirtieth anniversary, Buckley pointed out that the current issue of *NR* discussed the Geneva summit, the war in Afghanistan, Sandinista involvement in Colombia, the attrition of order and discipline in the public schools, and the underrated legacy of Herman Kahn. Some disengagement.

SDI was the cornerstone of Reagan's campaign to strengthen America's national defenses—so crucial to his plans that he would never accede to Gorbachev's repeated attempts to secure its abandonment. Among SDI's greatest friends, Bridges and Coyne write, were Bill Buckley and *National Review.* Buckley retained physicist Robert Jastrow to write a regular feature, "SDI Watch," which reported the ups and downs in the initiative's development and the mainstream media's attacks on it. Buckley understood that by forcing the Kremlin to expand resources to counter it, "SDI was a powerful force in the eventual dissolution of the Soviet empire."[29]

President Reagan may have had the last word about Bill Buckley being out of touch at the official opening (in February 1983) of *NR*'s first formal Washington office, headed by John McLaughlin, who went on to found and host the long-running television discussion program *The McLaughlin Group*. Addressing a happy band of conservative writers, activists, members of Congress, and administration officials, Reagan looked at Buckley and said, "There's a problem, though, Bill, that I think you should know about. It's all the talk about your being aloof and insensitive and an out-of-touch editor. People are saying that you spend too much time away from New York. They're also saying you're being pushed around by your staff. And I understand there's a new button on the market, 'Let Buckley Be Buckley.'"[30] The assembly roared with laughter, appreciating that conservatives had been complaining that White House aides were blocking the conservative agenda. A cry had gone up: "Let Reagan Be Reagan!"

That the two men enjoyed each other immensely can be seen from their vacation in April 1983 with wives Pat and Nancy at the Barbados villa of actress Claudette Colbert. While swimming the first day, Buckley asked Reagan if he wanted to earn the *National Review* Medal of Freedom. When the president asked what he had to do, Buckley replied, "Well, I will proceed to almost drown, and you will rescue me."[31] Reagan, who saved a recorded seventy-seven people from drowning during his summers as a young lifeguard in Dixon, Illinois, happily complied. Unfortunately, no photographer recorded the high jinks of America's two most famous conservatives.

Despite his fondness for the president, Buckley criticized him when he felt it necessary, as when 241 Marines were killed in the fall of 1983 by a suicide bomber who rammed a dynamite-filled truck into a barracks in Lebanon. What was their mission, Mr. President? the magazine asked. What mission could have been accomplished by so few men? The invasion of Grenada and the ousting of Marxist leader Maurice Bishop were another matter. Foreign-policy specialist Brian Crozier wrote in *NR* that the Brezhnev Doctrine was no more. "Soviet imperial power has been rolled back, if only to the extent of 100,000 people and 133 square miles. Not much? It is enormous in significance."[32]

In November 1984, Reagan won another landslide victory, carrying forty-nine states and receiving more than fifty million popular votes, the first presidential candidate in American history to do so. In an effusive postelection column, Buckley described Reagan as an "extraordinary president" who radiated an "idealistic self-assurance." He subsequently urged the president to move dramatically in a more conservative direction, freezing entitlements and creating a "defense shield in space." Reagan, who had voted for Franklin D. Roosevelt four times, preferred to approach the question of entitlements cautiously, focusing on the excesses of the Great Society but leaving Social Security alone. But he welcomed the idea of a space shield as part of SDI.[33]

In December 1985, Bill Buckley celebrated his sixtieth birthday and *National Review* its thirtieth anniversary with a black-tie and ball-gown banquet at the Plaza Hotel in New York City, featuring remarks by President Reagan. Senior editor Richard Brookhiser, who everyone assumed was being groomed to succeed Buckley, said that "in a hundred years, there is not a person or a thing in this room that will remain. But our ideas will remain." Several speakers, including Jeffrey Hart and Buckley, quoted Whittaker Chambers to reinforce Reagan's statement that the enemy America faced was an "evil empire." Reagan leaned toward Priscilla Buckley and whispered to her, "It *is* an evil empire."[34]

After detailing the advances of freedom around the world and the material role American conservatism had played, Reagan singled out *National Review*. We are gathered, he said, to "celebrate thirty years of witty, civilized pages from our beloved *National Review* and the damage, the terminal damages, those pages have done to modern statism and its unrelenting grimness." He saluted Buckley, "our clipboard-bearing Gallahad," "for setting loose so much good in the world. And, Bill," he said, "thanks, too, for all the fun."[35]

There were still miles to go for Ronald Reagan, who would oversee passage of the Tax Reform Act of 1986, lowering the top marginal income-tax rate from 50 percent to 33 percent and removing an estimated 4.3 million low-income families from the tax rolls; nominate to the Supreme Court the distinguished jurist Robert Bork, only to see the nominee undone by a snarling network of liberal organizations; and implement the Reagan Doctrine, which produced a Soviet pullout from Afghanistan, the election of a democratic government in Nicaragua, and the removal of forty thousand Cuban troops from Angola. And he would suffer through the Iran-contra "scandal," which was not Watergate redux but a gross mistake in judgment. As the Republican members of a select committee of the House and Senate that investigated the funds diversion stated, "There was no constitutional crisis, no systematic disrespect for the 'internal rule of law,' no grand conspiracy."[36]

Addressing the unprecedented propaganda campaign against Judge Bork, Buckley neatly summed up the preposterous case of Bork's critics in two short sentences: "What the opponents of Robert Bork are saying comes down to this: (1) We believe in an activist court that does not hesitate to write social policy. (2) But that social policy must be what we favor; for which reason, (3) Bork the legal scholar, the veteran teacher, administrator and judge, is not fit to serve."[37]

Although not a lawyer, Buckley possessed a love of logic and precise language found in the best jurists—which led him to comment on the constitutional debate surrounding Attorney General Edwin Meese III. In October 1986, Meese shocked many on the Left when he stated that a Supreme Court decision "does not establish 'a supreme law of the land' that is binding on all persons and parts of the government, henceforth and forever more."[38]

Meese was on firm legal ground. After all, Lincoln led a war to overturn the court's decision in *Dred Scott v. Sandford*, which said Congress could not stop slavery in the territories. Meese stated that there was a difference between constitutional law—the rulings of the court—and the Constitution. As Buckley wrote, "Edwin Meese . . . is asking merely that we (whether legislator, voter, pundit, or moralist) withhold judgment on the judicial, let alone moral, finality of a court ruling until it has survived the acquiescence of time. That is sound conservative thinking, of the kind that would surely have been welcomed by Dred Scott."[39]

One Reagan action that Buckley and *National Review* did not welcome was the Intermediate-Range Nuclear Forces (INF) Treaty with the Soviets. Buckley and Reagan wrote each other often and at length about the treaty, with Buckley raising strong objections and the president doing his best to reassure his old friend. In one letter, Buckley said bluntly, "SDI is not going to survive merely because you are in favor of it. Unhappily, it is, in my judgment, going to be spiked by Congress."[40]

Europeans with whom Buckley was in touch believed that the removal of land-based missiles in Western Europe that could reach Soviet territory—the end result of the INF treaty—would persuade the Soviets they could "safely proceed on the assumption that no American president is going to commit nuclear forces to stop a Soviet blitzkrieg." Buckley pointed out that it was not only "the far right" that was unhappy with the treaty. He mentioned Jeane Kirkpatrick and Henry Kissinger as among those who feared the consequences in "a post-Reagan age."[41]

"I still think we are on solid ground on the INF Treaty," the president responded, "based on our verification provisions and on the fact that Gorby knows what our response to cheating would be—it's spelled Pershing."[42] (That is, if the Soviets cheated, the United States would redeploy the Pershing II missiles based in Germany and Great Britain.)

The president had an extended telephone conversation with Buckley in the fall of 1987 in which he repeated several times that he was not, as some on the Right charged, going "soft." Rather, he said, "I'm determined that for the sake of the world we need if possible to eliminate nuclear weapons, but I am not going to do it at the expense of leaving us outweighted [*sic*] by them—and I haven't softened up a bit."⁴³

Despite Reagan's assurances, Buckley approved an *NR* cover that blared, "Reagan's Suicide Pact." The magazine warned that the treaty would destabilize Western Europe and leave it at the mercy of the Soviet Union. Anxious conservatives dismissed Reagan's mantra, "Trust, but verify." When the Berlin Wall fell in 1989 and the Soviet Union quietly dissolved two years later, the full impact of Reagan's "suicide pact" became clear. Buckley tacitly acknowledged his error in his 1995 novel, *A Very Private Plot,* in which a fictional Reagan muses in the Oval Office about his conservative friends who "sometimes don't see the important things." "And anyway," the president says to himself, "Gorbachev isn't giving away anything he isn't prepared to give away. He doesn't know how much I know about how much he's hurting. Wasteland, the Soviet economy."⁴⁴

In his farewell address in January 1989, President Reagan reassured the men and women of the Reagan Revolution that they had made a difference—they had made the nation stronger, freer, and had left it in good hands. "All in all," he said, with the suggestion of a twinkle in his eye, "not bad, not bad at all."⁴⁵ And then, having survived an assassin's bullet, a recession, Iran-contra, the "borking" of his Supreme Court nominee, the slings and arrows of outraged liberals about his tax cuts, and the alarums of nervous conservatives about his summit meetings with Gorbachev, he went home with a public approval rating of 63 percent, the highest of any retiring president up to that point.

Aside from the decline of the New Right—which often criticized Reagan more harshly than his Democratic opponents—the 1980s were generally bountiful years for conservatives across the country, as all the elements of a successful political movement came together: a consistent and relevant philosophy, a national constituency, requisite financing, a solid organizational base, media proficiency, and charismatic principled leadership. *National Review* reached a circulation high of 200,000. The Heritage Foundation doubled its annual budget to nearly $18 million. Charles Murray, Michael Novak, Dinesh D'Souza, George Gilder, and Marvin Olasky published influential bestselling books. Foundations like the Lynde and Harry Bradley Foundation, the John M. Olin Foundation, the Sarah Scaife Foundation, and the redoubtable Earhart Foundation disbursed millions of dollars each year to think tanks, academics, authors, and publications.

There were inevitable tensions within the movement as it grew in size and influence. In the 1950s the sharpest differences were between traditionalists and libertarians as to the right balance between liberty and order. In the 1980s traditionalists and neoconservatives argued over the proper role of the state. At the 1986 national meeting of the Philadelphia Society, conservative professor Stephen Tonsor deplored the "arrogance" of former Marxists and radicals—i.e., the neoconservatives—dictating policies and beliefs to those who had never strayed from the truth. There also sprouted up in the nation's capital a species of conservative careerists, drawn by the prospect of using political power to advance conservative goals and, even more importantly, themselves. Observing their eager wheeling and dealing, M. Stanton Evans remarked, "Too many conservatives come to Washington thinking that it is a cesspool and wind up thinking it is a hot tub."[46]

During the 1980s, the external threat of Communism and the calming presence of Ronald Reagan persuaded most conservatives to sublimate their differences for the greater good. But with the collapse of Communism in Eastern and Central Europe in 1989 and the dissolution of the Soviet Union in 1991—and the departure of the artful Reagan—disagreements between the varying kinds of conservatism became more intense.

STILL IN THE RING

Bill Buckley had no intention of leaving the public square, but as he approached sixty-five—the age when his father retired—he addressed the question of who should succeed him as editor of *National Review*, his most important and, he hoped, lasting contribution to the conservative movement and American politics. In 1987, Richard Brookhiser learned to his sharp disappointment that Buckley had changed his mind—he was no longer the designated successor.[47] Following a brief but intense period of consultation with colleagues and friends, Buckley settled on John O'Sullivan, a brilliant, witty Anglo-Irish editor who had run newspapers and journals on both sides of the Atlantic. At the time, O'Sullivan was a special adviser and sometime speechwriter for Prime Minister Margaret Thatcher.

NR's thirty-fifth anniversary in 1990 coincided with Buckley's sixty-fifth birthday, and as he had long planned,

Bill Buckley announced his retirement—after 1,014 issues—as editor-in-chief and turned over the helm to John O'Sullivan. There were more than a few tears and exclamations of protest among those in attendance at the traditional black-tie banquet. Do not despair, Buckley said, smiling, for he would not discontinue his column or *Firing Line* or public speaking or book writing. But prudence required him to arrange for the continuation of *National Review*, which, "I like to think, will be here, enlivening right reason, for as long as there is anything left in America to celebrate."[48]

Buckley's notion of "retirement" was anyone else's full-time job. He remained on the *NR* masthead as editor at large, which meant that while he would no longer lead the editorial meetings or edit the upfront section, "The Week," he would be available for consultation and would let the new editor know "if there was anything he disliked."[49] Once a year, until the mid-1990s, he took over the biweekly editorial meeting to remind everyone that the contents of the magazine remained of paramount importance to him.

In addition, he stayed busy with the weekly *Firing Line* (although in 1988 he had cut the program from an hour to a half hour), his syndicated column (which he reduced from three times to two times a week in 1994), his lectures (trimmed from seventy to about twenty a year), and his fiction and nonfiction books, ranging from novels about Joe McCarthy and Elvis Presley to a history of the rise and fall of the Berlin Wall. In November 1991, he received the Presidential Medal of Freedom—the nation's highest civilian award—from President George H. W. Bush, who said that "the United States honors . . . a tireless worker in the vineyards of liberty."[50]

Surveying Buckley's impact on American politics—including the peace dividend of the Cold War victory and the entrenchment of Reagan's domestic legacy under President Clinton—John O'Sullivan declared that Bill Buckley "had in effect achieved his political ambitions (astonishingly ambitious ones in 1951) more completely than any other major figure of his time."[51] That is hyperbolic—Reagan led the way at home and abroad—but Buckley's role in building the conservative movement was essential to Reagan's success.

Almost all of those who had been with Buckley when he founded *NR* in 1955 and as he built the conservative movement over the following thirty years were now gone. In July 1987, after several years of declining health, James Burnham died, prompting a sorrowing Buckley to write:

> I don't think any of my colleagues would question that the figure for whom they had the greatest respect, and to whom they felt the greatest sense of gratitude, was James Burnham, who was never too busy to give the reasons for thinking as he did, or too harassed to interrupt his own work to help others with theirs. His generosity was egregiously exploited by one person, whose only excuse, now, is that at least he has documented his gratitude by penning these words.[52]

Burnham was the last of the major intellectual and political influences on Buckley to pass away. There had been Albert Jay Nock, the acerbic antistatist whom he had first read and met as a teenager; Willmoore Kendall, the brilliant, disputatious traditionalist who had mentored him at Yale; Whittaker Chambers, the Communist spy turned eloquent anti-Communist who had served briefly as a senior editor of *National Review* in its first years; and Burnham, a former man of the Left whose pragmatism in politics and policy had guided Buckley for a quarter of a century. All four men were facets of the fusionist conservatism that Buckley personified and employed to shape the American conservative movement.

In April 1994 Russell Kirk passed away. Buckley paid tribute to the fluent historian and man of letters who with his seminal work *The Conservative Mind* gave the movement its name. He recalled that his association with Kirk was older than the life of *National Review,* stretching back to the fall of 1954, when he traveled to Piety Hill in the hill country of Michigan to persuade the conservative scholar to associate "his august name" with a new magazine. Kirk agreed and for the next twenty-five years wrote about higher education in America in *NR.* In the ensuing fourteen years, after he had discontinued the *NR* column, Kirk wrote numerous books and essays, gave speeches, and "influenced the lives of another half-generation." Few men, Buckley wrote fondly about his colleague and champion of ordered liberty, "have repaid their debt to their family, their country, and their faith so extravagantly."[53] He did not mention that Kirk had opposed the Persian Gulf War, which Buckley and the magazine endorsed, or that the Michigan native had served as state cochairman of Pat Buchanan's insurgent presidential bid in 1992.

Kirk and his traditionalist conservatism were on Buckley's mind when *National Review* celebrated its fortieth birthday in late 1995. Before discussing how to cope with the destructive legacy of seventy-five years of totalitarianism behind the Iron Curtain, Buckley said a few words about the role of fusionism in the development of modern American conservatism. When *NR* was launched in 1955, he said, two traditions were at odds, although not with daggers drawn: the libertarian and the traditionalist. The former was "anti-statist, pure and simple." The latter spoke of traditional values, calling for respect for our forefathers and mediating institutions such as the family, the church, and the courts.

Libertarian Frank Meyer was ultimately persuaded that "tradition was important to the good health of libertarian mores." Traditionalist Russell Kirk acknowledged that the state was "the presumptive enemy of useful social energy, as the predicable obstacle to liberal progress." The two schools came together in *National Review,* Buckley said, which "gave enthusiastic shelter to advocates of both." The meeting of such minds as those of Meyer and Kirk "grew to be known as Fusionism; and little fusionists were born and baptized from coast to coast."[54] Although he did not say it, Buckley was the godfather of both ceremonies.

As to whether the future would take Americans "into a better world, with reduced government," or to "a kind of Orwellian transcription of democracy," we cannot be certain, Buckley said. We do know, he added, that "history triumphant awaits the crystallization of an informed public intelligence seeking maximum human freedom." The easiest way for history to take its cue "is to maintain its subscription to *National Review.*"[55]

In 1998, halfway through the second term of President Bill Clinton—who had provided abundant and pungent copy for *National Review*—John O'Sullivan stepped down as *NR* editor after nearly a decade, and was replaced by the young, politically attuned Rich Lowry, the magazine's national political reporter. In the words of biographers Bridges and Coyne, O'Sullivan had "done much to raise the magazine's profile . . . and bring [its] operations into the late twentieth century." He had hired the well-connected Kate O'Beirne away from the Heritage Foundation and installed gifted young writers like Lowry and the always insightful Ramesh Ponnuru. O'Sullivan displayed a flair for organizing, holding "fusionist" conferences in Washington and elsewhere at which traditional conservatives, libertarians, neoconservatives, and even a few liberals discussed the future of conservatism.[56]

Lowry recalls that he and Buckley had a one-hour luncheon at the Hay-Adams Hotel in Washington, D.C., at which they discussed the future of *National Review.* Buckley was convinced that the magazine needed "a new burst of energy," undoubtedly conscious of the increased competition from the recently launched *Weekly Standard,* which was all Washington politics, all the time. Buckley had always had an eye for young talent, and Lowry's keen political writing had caught his eye. Following their Washington luncheon, Buckley called Lowry and said, somewhat playfully, "I'm going to swing with you." Rich Lowry was twenty-nine, the same age as Bill Buckley when he launched *National Review.*[57]

Lowry benefited from Buckley's patience, especially in the first year, as when he admitted he had scheduled an article titled "Bomb Canada" in the same issue that the advertising director, after months of effort, had obtained an advertisement from the U.S.-Canada Friendship Coun-

cil. The young editor readily conceded that Buckley oper-
ated on a higher intellectual plane. When Buckley said that
an article was characterized by an "unnecessary anfractu-
osity," Lowry nodded and said, "You know, I couldn't agree
with you more."[58]

Aided by Buckley, the new editor took command. He
surrounded himself with talented youthful conservatives
like Jay Nordlinger and John Miller. He started up the enormously successful National Review Online and installed
Jonah Goldberg and the energetic Kathryn Lopez, a graduate of the Catholic University of America, as editors. Under
Lowry's editorship, *NR* continued to be the voice of mainstream American conservatism.

National Review warned repeatedly in 1998 that Republicans should not neglect hard issues like school choice,
Social Security privatization, and the passage of "emer-
gency" spending bills in favor of an almost lascivious focus
on President Clinton's personal misbehavior and forth-
coming impeachment. When the Senate in February 1999
failed to convict Clinton of high crimes and misdemeanors,
recriminations among conservatives flowed hot and heavy.
How could we have let him get away with it? they demanded
of each other. Rich Lowry, in his carefully researched Clinton study, *Legacy,* argues, "There were two overriding factors that would ultimately save Clinton in the Lewinsky
affair: his wife and a broad cultural shift in the American
public that predisposed it to go easy on him."[59]

In several speeches during the impeachment proceed-
ings, Bill Buckley coolly analyzed why the American people
had not been more outraged by behavior that even Clinton's most eloquent defender, former Democratic senator

Dale Bumpers, characterized as "indefensible, outrageous, unforgivable, and shameless."[60] Elaborating on Lowry's explanation, Buckley offered several propositions, raising the issue to a higher intellectual level:

"Many Americans seemed to be saying that public servants can be expected to be—casual—in the matter of conjugal morality."

"Whatever the concern for morality and integrity, the political consideration inevitably figures."

"America is correctly proud of its capacity to forgive, but also we are aware that forgiveness is a joint exercise."

The public, Buckley noted, "does not seem to be determined to exact convincing contrition." "What is the matter with the public?" he asked. "Why does it not understand the gravity of what is happening?" Some might say, he suggested, that "for most Americans, conduct, unless it directly affects them, is no longer evaluated by what were once publicly acknowledged as public standards."

But he firmly rejected any such triumph of what some might call "personal detachment" and followers of Ayn Rand would term "the triumph of self-concern." "The task ahead," Buckley averred, "is to reconstruct our basic allegiance to what is right"—an always prime objective of *National Review* and its founding editor.

Pressed for years to write a "Catholic" book, Bill Buckley at last produced in 1997 *Nearer, My God: An Autobiography of Faith*, which William J. Bennett, a Catholic, called "a modern pilgrim's progress" and Charles W. Colson, a Protestant, praised as a "deeply personal defense of his Catholic faith."[61] It is filled with the erudite opinions of friends and colleagues about Catholicism and its many strengths and weaknesses but sparse as to the intimate details of the author's faith—except in two places.

Buckley traveled to Lourdes in 1994 not to seek a miraculous cure of a physical ailment—he was in comparatively good health at the time—but to satisfy his curiosity about "what exactly goes on there and what its impact might be on one first-time visitor." He left Lourdes deeply, profoundly touched by the faith of the thousands of *malades* who came hoping but not expecting a miracle and who came away with "a sense of reconciliation, if not well-being." "Our burden," he writes, "is to keep the faith" whatever God's plan for us, knowing that "the greatest tonic of all is divine love, which is nourished by human love, even as human love is nourished by divine love."[62]

The most personal chapter is the one about the ordination of Michael Bozell, the son of his sister Patricia (Trish) Bozell, to whom he was closest of all his brothers and sisters. The chapter is prime Buckley, overflowing with descriptions of the fifty-one relatives and friends who expectantly traveled to the Benedictine abbey of Solesmes in northern France for Brother Michael's ordination, the truly awful wine at the party the night before (alas, there was no miracle and the water remained water), a moving letter read by father Brent (now in a wheelchair) to son Michael, and a description of the monastery with its "unmistakable feel and aroma of age and piety and indomitability."

Lying in his snug hotel bed and thinking of the young monk in his cell rising at midnight to sing his orisons, Buckley concluded that almost certainly Michael "was the happiest of us all, and that only God can dispense such a [thing] as that."[63]

In June 1998, Senator Barry Goldwater of Arizona, the most influential loser in modern presidential politics, died at the age of eighty-seven, prompting a Buckley obituary detailing the Arizonan's stubborn individualism in politics and life and his manifold contributions to American conservatism. Buckley quoted liberal Hubert Humphrey: "Barry, you're one of the handsomest men in America. You ought to be in the movies. In fact, I've made just that proposal to Eighteenth Century Fox." Buckley speculated that Goldwater probably smiled at the jest, but others, particularly on the Right, would venture that back in the eighteenth century, "Barry Goldwater would have been more at home at the Convention in Philadelphia than most modern liberals."[64]

In early 1983, a perplexed Goldwater had written Buckley to inquire what he had done to "bring down the wrath" of Young Americans for Freedom and other conservative groups. Buckley gently explained that it was the senator's pro-choice stance on abortion and his "resolute opposition to any legislative efforts to cure the usurpations of the [Supreme] Court." Nevertheless, he reassured his conservative colleague, "your own place in history is very secure."[65]

In October 1999, the man who had been given a hundred awards in his life accepted yet another—the Clare Boothe Luce Award of the Heritage Foundation. This was a signal honor by reason of the person for whom the award was named—Clare Boothe Luce, as witty, provocative, and Catholic as the recipient—and the person who introduced him, son Christopher, who concluded his introduction by saying:

I've watched the president of the United States hang a medal around his neck and call him a hero. I've listened as Cardinal O'Connor . . . addressed him in a room crowded with important prelates and called him "the jewel in the crown of American Catholicism." And I have heard my mother say one thousand times, "Your father is impossible."

And you know, they were all right.[66]

Buckley did not wait until the millennium to take his next steps into retirement. In December 1999 he brought the inestimable *Firing Line* to a close. For thirty-three years, it had maintained an unmatched level of intellectual discourse on television. The program still holds the record as the longest-running public-affairs television show with a single host.

At about the same time, Buckley announced his retirement from the lecture circuit, although he continued to speak—without a fee—before conservative organizations like the Philadelphia Society, the Intercollegiate Studies Institute, and *National Review.*

In June 2004, he relinquished his controlling shares of *NR* to a preselected board of trustees: his son, Christopher; Thomas L. (Dusty) Rhodes, the magazine's president; Ed Capano, the publisher; Evan Galbraith, his old sailing friend from Yale and former ambassador to France; Daniel Oliver, former chairman of the Federal Trade Commission; and Austin Bramwell, a 2000 Yale graduate and one of *NR*'s youngest contributors.

But Buckley continued to write his column and turn out books at a rate that would intimidate a normal

author—or indeed several of them. The same year he relinquished control of the magazine, he published a concise
history of an epic event, *The Fall of the Berlin Wall,* as well
as *Miles Gone By,* a literary autobiography containing previ-
ously published essays he had chosen, arranged, and newly
edited. *Miles Gone By* wound up on the *New York Times*
bestseller list, unusual for a collection of already published
work. Buckley also submitted the manuscript of *Last Call
for Blackford Oakes* for publication in the spring of 2005.
From the very first to the last Oakes novel, the fixed philosophical star of their hero was the ideals of America. "Any
failure by beneficiaries of the free world," wrote Buckley,
"to recognize what we have here over against what it is [the
communists] would impose on us, amounts to a moral and
intellectual nihilism."[67]

In June 2004, a decade after revealing he had Alzheimer's, Ronald Reagan quietly slipped away. The death of any
president is momentous, but the passing of America's fortieth president at the age of ninety-three evoked seven days
of national remembrance, sorrow, and affection not seen
since the assassination of John F. Kennedy in November
1963 and the wartime death of Franklin Delano Roosevelt
in April 1945.

National Review devoted a memorial issue to Reagan,
a faithful reader of the magazine almost from its founding
and in later years a member of its board of directors. Bill
Buckley contributed two essays so devotional as almost to
be embarrassing, but there was no hint of embarrassment
in Buckley, who compared Reagan to Lincoln, both of their
lives "mythogenic beginning to end."

Of Reagan's foreign policy, Buckley wrote, the "conclusive factor in the matter of American security against any threat of Soviet aggression" was the character of the man in the White House, Ronald Reagan, who did not hesitate to label the Soviet Union an "evil empire." Here at home, Buckley added, Reagan told us that "most of our civic problems were problems brought on or exacerbated by government, not problems that could be solved by government." Reagan was scornful of the claims of omnipotent government, Buckley wrote, because "he felt, and expressed, the buoyancy of the American Republic."[68]

The great heroes of the 1980s, Buckley said, were Lech Walesa, Aleksandr Solzhenitsyn, and Andrei Sakharov, who earned their place in "freedom's House of Lords," but the political leader was Ronald Reagan, with his strategic vision.[69]

Reagan himself had already dubbed Bill Buckley a hero of freedom when he said, at *National Review's* thirtieth-anniversary party, that he remembered "a time when nightmare and danger reigned and only the knights of darkness prevailed." And then riding up came "our clipboard-bearing Galahad," who with grace and humor and passion raised "a standard to which patriots and lovers of freedom could repair."[70]

CHAPTER 5

LAST THINGS

No American president in his first year was as coolly welcomed and then as warmly praised by the public as George W. Bush. His beginning was overshadowed by the disputed nature of his 2000 victory—narrowly losing the popular vote to Democrat Al Gore and winning the Electoral College by just one vote more than the needed 270.

Widely described—and not only by partisan Democrats—as the man who "stole" the election, a cautious Bush began his presidency by focusing on taxes and education as evidence of his "compassionate conservatism." Bill Buckley frequently said of Bush, "He's conservative, but not *a* conservative."[1] Unease on the Right about the president increased commensurate with his willingness to be called a big-government conservative.

And then on September 11, 2001, four hijacked airplanes tore into the silver towers of the World Trade Center in New York City, the mammoth Pentagon in Washington, D.C., and the verdant Pennsylvania countryside, killing some three thousand people. The widespread discontent engendered by Bush's presidential nanovictory was swept aside by the violence of the Islamic terrorists. The nation was no longer divided into red states and blue states, but united in red, white, and blue, if temporarily.

President Bush moved aggressively to rally Congress, America's overseas allies, and the public. Aided by the public's historic tendency to rally around the president in a time of crisis as well as by his own decisive leadership, Bush's approval ratings skyrocketed until they reached 90 percent, the highest level of any president since the advent of polling. Only his father, George H. W. Bush, had approached the heights of such public approval, receiving a rating of 89 percent right after the successful conclusion of the Persian Gulf War in 1991.

An emboldened George W. Bush and his administration, led by Vice President Richard Cheney and Defense Secretary Donald Rumsfeld, promised to oust the Taliban government in Afghanistan, put terrorist leader Osama bin Laden on the run, and take appropriate action against Saddam Hussein in Iraq. An intense national debate ensued in the following months: what governmental actions were justified in this new and different kind of war—the war on terrorism?

For the conservative movement, there was another question: would the war on terrorism be the clarifying issue that united the varying strains of conservatism as the threat of Soviet Communism had during the Cold War? Ever protective of the movement he had created and nurtured for five decades, Bill Buckley addressed the war in a series of nuanced columns and interviews that blended the conservative, neoconservative, and sometimes even the paleoconservative position. It would be his last substantive public-policy contribution to American conservatism.

First came an emphatic call for action; then a reflective reevaluation; next an open admission that although military action against the terrorists in Afghanistan and Iraq had been justified, the continuing war in Iraq threatened not only the fortunes of the Bush administration but American conservatism; and finally qualified support for the 2007 surge and a resolution to "stick it out" in Iraq. While he supported the forcible removal of Saddam Hussein, Buckley viewed the attempted nation-building in Iraq to be a Wilsonian, and not a conservative, strategy. To his disappointment and dismay, Iraq did not unite conservatives but divided them—as it did the nation.

In the immediate aftermath of 9/11, Buckley and *National Review* strongly agreed about the course of action that America should take, but his skepticism about Iraq surfaced sooner than that of Rich Lowry and the other *NR* editors.

On September 14, just three days after the terrorist attacks, Buckley wrote that "a decisive confrontation" was justified and that "the theater for this is Iraq." Given Saddam Hussein's known willingness to develop and when necessary use "atomic-biological-chemical weapons," he said, the United States should give the following word to Saddam: "We are coming into Baghdad. We will arrive in force together with Pakistani, Egyptian and Russian military units. Your aggressive war of 1990 and your shelter of terrorist units ever since make you an enemy."

"From now on," Buckley wrote, anticipating what President Bush would say, "enemies who are associated with terrorist activity will not cohabit the globe with the United States."[2]

On October 5, four weeks after the destruction of the World Trade Center, Buckley wrote that "something more than the head of bin Laden is required to short-circuit the grid that binds the terrorists in their envious, fanatical designs on the free world." What was needed, he declared, was "the head of Saddam Hussein . . . the dogged and impenitent cultivator of apocalyptic weaponry."[3]

Four days later, Buckley took on the argument of fellow conservative Robert Novak that the United States should not strike against Saddam Hussein without "concrete evidence" that he was involved in the September 11 massacre. Buckley was not impressed by Saddam's disavowal of the 9/11 attacks: "So? Osama bin Laden *also* disavowed it, while congratulating the enterprise of its perpetrators." While conceding that the evidence in hand against Saddam's Iraq was "not what we would need in a court of law," Buckley said that "we would not, in 1942, "have been able to prove that Adolf Hitler was exterminating the Jews."

He counseled proceeding on the reasonable grounds that Saddam: (1) sheltered terrorists; (2) had attempted genocide; (3) had invaded Kuwait; and (4) had "slaughtered dissidents and cultivates the final weapons of war." There was no denying, Buckley wrote, that Iraq was "aligned with a force—a brotherhood—that under the banner of Islam makes war against us."

In the face of these facts, he said, America "does not need conclusive evidence of Iraq's participation in anti-

U.S. terrorism to issue an ultimatum: Open your borders to an uninhibited inspection of Iraqi recesses of terrorist and aggressive activity."[4]

In June 2002, *NR* editor Rich Lowry echoed Buckley's militant language, calling for "a liberated Iraq" that would produce "a fresh start for the region." He cited approvingly the Bush administration's ambition, which he described as "an effort to remake politics in the entire Middle East in a new reformist, free-market, pluralistic direction." That effort, Lowry wrote, "has to start with something entirely new, a clean slate—in other words, a post-Saddam Iraq." A liberated Iraq would mean that Iran would be surrounded by states friendly to the United States, Syria would be cut off from Iraqi and Iranian trade, and "the U.S. will have new leverage over the Saudis."[5]

In September 2002, commenting on President Bush's address to the United Nations about Iraq's failure to comply with a long series of UN resolutions, Buckley set forth the U.S. position: "Saddam Hussein *has* chemical and biological weapons. Not prospectively, but in hand." He then quoted Bush's six-point ultimatum to Saddam, which concluded, "The just demands of peace and security will be met, *or action will be unavoidable.*"

During the Bush speech, Buckley noted, the camera turned from time to time to a stony-faced Iraqi ambassador to the UN. Behind him, an aide "who might have been Saddam's brother chewed gum." Everybody in the UN, Buckley wrote, "has chewed gum for years, including the U.S. delegation. But no longer, Mr. Bush has said."[6]

Buckley's strong approval of the president's ultimatum to Saddam Hussein was clear, and just as clear was his assumption—based on the assertions and evidence offered by the Bush administration, including Colin Powell's compelling address to the UN—that Saddam had in hand and was willing to use weapons of mass destruction. Buckley's support of the removal of Saddam Hussein was also predicated on the consequences of the U.S. failure to do so in the first Gulf War. As Buckley wrote, "we know now that we made a serious mistake in failing to consummate the [Persian Gulf] war we had engaged in under brilliant political and military leadership."[7]

In May 2003, he took up the question of whether the Iraq War was a just war, quoting extensively from remarks by President Bush. He listed the criteria: "It had to be that the offense was critical, that the defense was appropriate, that the violence was proportional." Buckley accepted Bush's descriptions of U.S. actions in Afghanistan and Iraq as "proportionate to the offense," and said that the president now had "history itself to point to, to the effect that what needs to be done to target terrorists and their supporters we can do without open, or unspoken, or furtive fear that superseded canons of moral restraint will enfeeble our resolution, and distract our purpose."[8] To put it more simply, the Iraq War was a just war.

But Iraq continued to divide conservatives. In the spring of 2003, *National Review* featured a cover article by David Frum (a former speechwriter for President George W. Bush), who declared war on paleoconservatives, calling them "unpatriotic" conservatives who should be read out of the movement for "turning their backs on their country" and failing to support the war on terrorism. David Keene, chairman of the American Conservative Union, responded that Frum had painted "with far too broad a brush" and that while he supported the war in Iraq, he did not like "nation-building" (a position Bill Buckley would come to adopt).[9]

As the rhetoric escalated, veteran conservatives such as Donald Devine (who headed the Office of Personnel Management under President Reagan) called for a return to Frank Meyer's fusionist conservatism. But it was not to be. Commentator Patrick Buchanan, representing the Old Right, vociferously opposed the war and U.S. "occupation" of Iraq. William Kristol, the resourceful editor of the neoconservative *Weekly Standard,* as strongly supported the war and a policy of preemptive action against terrorism when and where necessary (not excluding Iran).

FOLLOWING BURKE

Reacting to the intensifying debate, Owen Harries, the former editor of the neoconservative *National Interest,* offered some advice from the British conservative Edmund Burke about the dangers of overreaching in foreign policy. "We may say that we shall not abuse this astonishing and hitherto unheard of power," Burke wrote of the colossus-like British Empire in the 1770s, prior to the American Revolution. "But every other nation will think we shall abuse it. It is impossible but that, sooner or later, this state of things must produce a combination against us which may end in ruin."[10]

Buckley, who had come to know Burke through Russell Kirk, took the British statesman's warning to heart. By

July 2004, as American military and Iraqi civilian casualties mounted, and no light at the end of the tunnel had yet appeared, Buckley's enthusiasm for the war had disappeared, replaced by a determination to take lessons from "what has gone wrong in Iraq." President Bush, he said, would do "well to acknowledge the weaknesses in the course of action he took."[11]

To delineate those weaknesses, Buckley turned to an essay by Boston University professor Andrew Bacevich in the *American Conservative,* a paleoconservative journal founded by Patrick Buchanan. Bacevich argued that American policy makers had a disposition to "Wilsonian illusion" and had exchanged "the limited burdens of containment for the far more onerous burdens of occupation." Anticipating the debate over the forces needed for successful suppression of terrorism, Bacevich wrote, "The margin of U.S. military supremacy is thinner than advertised." Consider the possibility, said the West Point graduate and academic, "that bringing democracy to the Arab world is akin to making bricks without straw." Buckley wrote that President Bush needed to "dwell on these points," as the consequences of the Iraq War would affect "American politics for years to come."

Buckley could have cited, but did not, a sober *National Review* editorial that pointed out that the Iraqi insurgency had remained stubbornly strong and that the Bush administration "clearly wasn't ready for the magnitude of the task that rebuilding and occupying Iraq would present." While insisting that Iraq was not a "neoconservative" war but "a war of national interest," the editorial urged the United States to downplay expectations. "If we leave Iraq in some sort of orderly condition," said the editors, "with some sort of legitimate non-dictatorial government and a roughly working economy, we will be doing very well." Gone with the wind was any suggestion of nation-building.[12]

Buckley followed his increasing skepticism about the war to what he considered to be a logical conclusion. In a June 2004 *New York Times* interview he said: "With the benefit of minute hindsight, Saddam Hussein wasn't the kind of extra-territorial menace that was assumed by the administration one year ago. If I knew then what I know now about what kind of situation we would be in, I would have opposed the war."[13]

Days later, Buckley wrote a column in response to the criticism his comments had generated. Some conservatives, Buckley wrote, believed that he was being "disloyal to a cause," others that he was giving the Democrats "prime bait for exploitation" in a presidential election year. He explained his objections to the Iraqi incursion—that Saddam did not have "a handy supply of weapons of mass destruction," as the Bush administration had stated, and that "the responsibility for rebuilding Iraq politically . . . should have been done by others, with support from the United States." "Knocking off Saddam Hussein" was one thing, he wrote; rebuilding Iraq was quite another.[14]

Buckley's shift on the Iraq War was noted by the paleoconservatives but did not earn him any plaudits. Where was he when he was needed, they asked, when the decision to go to war was made? Ultralibertarian Lew Rockwell fairly screamed that the "conservatism created by William Buckley . . . gave us the most raw and stupid form of imperial big government one can imagine."[15] Neoconservatives were dismayed by Buckley's reversal but for the most part did not publicly express any sense of betrayal. Buckley did, however, have an emotional confrontation with Norman Podhoretz on an *NR* cruise, according to a bystander. When Podhoretz called the Iraq War "an amazing success," Buckley responded, "Aren't you embarrassed by the absence of these weapons [of mass destruction]?"[16]

In June 2005, the *NR* editors offered a multipoint argument in favor of the Iraq War, which they called a requisite front in the larger war against terrorism. They made their case by noting that (1) Saddam's regime had "a web of connections" to Islamic extremists and terrorists; (2) bin Laden had called Iraq a "crucial front" in the war on terror; (3) losing the Iraq War could result in a Sunni "rump state" that would be a haven for terrorists; and (4) a failure in Iraq would be a blow to America's prestige.[17]

Buckley was not persuaded. In September 2005, approaching *NR*'s fiftieth anniversary, George Will interviewed Bill Buckley for ABC's *This Week*. Buckley responded to a question about "nation-building" by saying that such a Wilsonian idea was "not at all conservative. It's anything but conservative." Conservatism, he said, "insists on coming to terms with the world as it is. . . . One recognizes that you can't export democracy everywhere simultaneously." The idea that a government that can't run Amtrak can run the Middle East, he told Will, is "an effrontery that both of us are familiar with."[18]

A month later, in an interview conducted shortly before his eightieth birthday, Buckley was still grappling with the war, reasserting that the U.S. enterprise in Iraq was "anything but conservative" but then adding, in a qualification of an earlier position, "This isn't to say that the war is wrong, or that history will judge it to be wrong. But it is absolutely to say that conservatism implies a certain submission to reality; and this war has an unrealistic frank and is being conscripted by events."[19] The "unrealistic frank" could only mean nation-building.

Buckley also expressed his disappointment with the state of American conservatism and remarked that it had "become a little bit slothful" in the absence of a galvanizing challenge like the Soviet Union during the Cold War. The resulting "attenuations" in the movement, he said, "haven't been resolved very persuasively." But he expressed guarded confidence that the conservative movement would undergo the same kind of intellectual reinvigoration that *National Review* had spurred in its early years. Reaching into his lexicon, he added, enigmatically, "*Mutatis mutandis*" (the necessary changes having been made).[20] Neither in this interview nor anywhere else in the public record did he say, as Jeffrey Hart subsequently claimed, that the conservative movement had "destroyed" itself by supporting the war in Iraq.[21]

While his disillusion with the war was profound, he told Van Galbraith, his closest personal friend and a firm supporter of the war, "Nothing would delight me more than to be wrong about this." He did not think he was. In January 2007, pretending to be a member of Congress, Buckley wrote that after considering all possible factors—from the loss of American lives and the impact of withdrawal on the "Iran question" to the continuing divisiveness of the Iraqis—he would "vote against supplementary American involvement in Iraq"—that is, against a "surge" in American troops proposed by General David Petraeus.[22]

However, in September 2007, in a column titled "Iraq: One More Time," Buckley asked a critical question then confronting Congress: what will happen in Iraq if America withdraws? In the very last sentence, he answered: "If the vote were mine, I'd say: Stick it out. You can't, by doing so, be accused of thoughtlessness, certainly not of perfidy." His counsel to "stick it out" was Bill Buckley's last public comment about the Iraq War.

His argument that the Bush strategy of nation-building in Iraq was utopian in nature—and fated to fail—was at last accepted by *NR*'s editor. In a column titled "The End of Illusion II," Rich Lowry wrote, "One of the era's great illusions was spun by President Bush—that the force of freedom was so irresistible, it would prevail in a place like Iraq even in the absence of law and order."[23]

Given President Bush's temperament, however, it is doubtful he would have abandoned his illusions even if he had paid more attention to Bill Buckley.

Paying His Debt

Reagan speechwriter Peter Robinson recalls the time he spent with Buckley in Switzerland as a researcher. "Bill," he said one day, "you were born wealthy and you've been famous for thirty years. Why do you keep working so hard?"

"WFB looked at me, surprised. 'My father taught me that I owe it to my country,' he replied. 'It's how I pay my debt.'"[24]

Buckley felt so strongly about the idea of personal obligation—set forth in 1973 in *Four Reforms*—that in 1990 he wrote a little book, *Gratitude: Reflections on What We Owe to Our Country,* in which he proposed a plan for voluntary national service of one year for men and women eighteen years and older. Nock would have been outraged, but Kendall, Chambers, and Burnham would have approved Buckley's federalist approach. Under the Buckley plan, the fifty states would approve the various programs; pay the volunteers with state, not federal, funds; and monitor the young people's activities. But there would be a federal agency that would set general standards—endorsing care for the aged over teaching children how to swim—and enforce sanctions such as denying federal aid to any college-bound student who did not have a national service certificate. If the plan took hold, he wrote, "the appetite to contribute to the health and morale of the republic would endure." It was only sensible to expect, he said, "that a sense of solidarity with one's fellow citizens, a sharpened esprit de corps will survive the initial term of service."[25]

He personally kept paying his debt to his nation and the movement he formed—through opulent celebrations of *NR*'s fiftieth anniversary and his eightieth birthday (President George W. Bush hosted a luncheon at the White House); through the deaths of old friends and colleagues like Hugh Kenner, Nicola Paone (owner of Buckley's favorite New York City restaurant), John Kenneth Galbraith, and Milton Friedman; through his own illness and increasingly poor health (diabetes, emphysema, and sleep apnea); and through the most crushing loss of all, Pat Buckley's passing.

In a brief *National Review* obituary, Buckley silhou-etted the sparkling life, the intimate partnership he had shared with Patricia Taylor Buckley. "It was she—all but uniquely she," he wrote, "who brought . . . the legion of guests, of all ages, professions, and interests, whose com-pany made up her lively life." Looking ahead to a life with-out Pat, he quoted a friend, a confirmed nonbeliever, who said that "for once I would like to be mistaken, and hope that, for you, this is not goodbye, but *hasta luego.*" Buckley responded, "No alternative thought would make continu-ing in life, for me, tolerable."[26]

In a December 2007 column, he explained the cause of his emphysema: "Half a year ago my wife died, technically from an infection, but manifestly, at least in part, from a body weakened by 60 years of nonstop smoking. I stayed off the cigarettes but went to the idiocy of cigars inhaled and suffer now from emphysema." And then Buckley, who often described himself as a libertarian, ended with these surprising words: "Stick me in a confessional and ask the question: Sir, if you had the authority, would you forbid smoking in America? You'd get a solemn and contrite, Yes."[27]

Earlier that year, slowed by what he called "my enfeeblement," he nevertheless took the long train ride from Stamford to Washington, D.C., to attend a dinner celebrating the dedication of the Victims of Communism Memorial and to receive the Truman-Reagan Medal of Freedom. Anti-Communist to the last, he came because an old friend asked him.

In what may have been his last public speech, Buck-ley talked about the importance of remembering the manifold crimes of Communism with "its ideology of ball and chain," as well as the "heroes of history" who bravely resisted its imposition. He spoke glowingly about the film *The Lives of Others,* which he called a "German master-piece"; the movie, set in East Berlin in the mid-1980s, tells the story of a veteran Stasi agent who is so moved by the courage of a young dissident couple that he does not report their "treason" to his superiors.[28]

The favor extended to a fellow member of the conservative movement was just one of many over the years. Asked by Father Robert Sirico, a young Catholic priest whom he had never met or corresponded with, to be the main speaker at the first public event of the Acton Institute in Grand Rapids, Michigan, Buckley said he would be delighted and waived his speaking fee. He was taken with the idea of an organization dedicated to explaining the relationship between free-market capitalism and Christian morality. He encouraged Frank Gaffney to start the neoconservative Center for Security Policy and helped with its fundraising. The very week he passed away he sent a substantial gift to Young America's Foundation, which had purchased and saved from the grasp of land developers Rancho del Cielo, the "Western White House" of the president he most admired—Ronald Reagan.

And there were his manifold acts of personal charity. He once visited a young man in a Texas hospital recovering from wounds incurred in Vietnam. The soldier's doctors had told him he would never see again. Buckley paid for his flight to New York City, where after an examination by one of the world's leading eye surgeons and three operations, the young veteran's eyesight was restored. Learning that a friend had written several Christmas songs for children, Buckley had them orchestrated and presented in concert— to a delighted audience of children.

Pondering on what would constitute an appropriate gift for his secretary Gertrude Vogt when she retired to hilly San Francisco, Buckley arranged with the Yellow Cab company to give her a permanent "free ride" in any of its cabs.[29] When veteran switchboard operator Rose Flynn celebrated her fiftieth anniversary with *National Review* in 2005, Buckley was in a hospital bed with the flu, half-delirious, but nevertheless dictated detailed memos about the planned party for Flynn.[30]

Like a modern Johnny Appleseed, he planted the seeds of friendship everywhere. Terry Eastland, the publisher of the *Weekly Standard* and before that the *American Spectator,* wrote in 1976 to Buckley with a question about Albert Jay Nock. Eastland was as unknown as Buckley was famous—a young writer who had just gotten his first newspaper job. But back came a letter, dictated in Switzerland, in which Buckley answered the question and then added, "That was a splendid essay you did on C. S. Lewis." Eastland was stunned—his essay had appeared eight months earlier in R. Emmett Tyrrell's *Alternative.* It was in fact Eastland's first published article. That his hero Bill Buckley had liked it was "a huge encouragement to someone toiling in the newspaper equivalent of low-A ball." There ensued a friendship of thirty years in which the personal get-togethers were infrequent but the notes and letters were many. "He was critically important," Eastland later wrote, "for those of us who came up in the fevered sixties and then had to endure the seventies, for he helped to make our way athwart history to the better time of the Reagan years."[31]

Until the end, Buckley expressed intense concern about the conservative movement, remarking in a November 2007 interview that the "conservative revolution" had "peaked" with Ronald Reagan's victory in 1980. Since then and even before, he said, conservatism seemed to have forgotten the libertarian message of Albert Jay Nock's *Our Enemy, the State*—"the consequences of which we have yet to pay for." It was a clear reference to the metastasizing of the federal government under President George W. Bush in domestic areas far removed from the legitimate war on terrorism. While it is not fair to say that "we have lost [the] war" against the welfare state, Buckley argued, "it is correct to say that it's a war that we need to continue to fight and concern ourselves with."[32]

In early February 2008, after more than five thousand of them, he sat down before his PC in his cluttered garage-office at Wallacks Point and wrote his last column. The subject: the obligation, particularly if you are in public life, to use the right words.

The occasion was a political debate between two Democratic presidential candidates—Hillary Clinton and Barack Obama. To put himself and the reader in the right mood, Buckley turned to Fowler's classic work, *Modern English Usage*, and gave examples of words in vogue (*ambience, protagonist, seminal*), words that were variants on a more common word (*adumbrate* for *sketch*, *liquidate* for *destroy*), scientific words "brought carelessly into general use" (*exponential growth, psychological moment*), and words of rhetorical appeal (*archetypal, massive, unthinkable*).[33]

Buckley was echoing George Orwell's famous 1945 essay "Politics and the English Language," in which the British novelist condemned staleness of imagery and lack of precision. Increasingly in political discourse, Orwell wrote, prose consists less and less of words chosen for the sake of their meaning and more of phrases "tacked together like the sections of a pre-fabricated hen-house."[34] Buckley acknowledged his debt to Orwell by titling the column "Fowlerspeak—Goodspeak."

Turning to Clinton and Obama, Buckley wrote that while both were intelligent and resourceful, they struck him as "absolutely uninterested in the vector of political force." Both contenders, he said, should spend time "on the problem of omnipotent government" and speak "the kind of language Fowler preached and preached in." It was good advice for all political contenders, regardless of party or the office sought.

It was his last column, but not his last word. Restless as ever, he had decided to write memoirs about two of the most influential conservatives of the twentieth century— Barry Goldwater and Ronald Reagan.

In August 2007, he completed *Flying High*, which concentrates on the 1960s, when Goldwater's forthright enunciation of conservative ideas inspired thousands of young people to take an interest in politics. The book captures the dramatic response Goldwater's 1964 presidential campaign inspired, as at a pre-nomination rally in San Francisco, when an ecstatic audience of college students declared opposition to their professors' "intensive indoctrination in state welfarism, anti-anti-Communism, moral libertinage, skepticism, anti-Americanism."[35] Buckley also captures the elation and the anxiety of the candidate and his campaign team as they made their way through the deep snows of New Hampshire, the fertile fields of Illinois, and the acrid haze of Los Angeles in pursuit of the GOP nomination and then the presidency. *Flying High* is Buckley's fond farewell to a politician who, by refusing to compromise his principles, offered a stirring profile in courage and candor.

In the book, Buckley quotes approvingly from Goldwater's *The Conscience of a Conservative*: "The government must begin to withdraw from a whole series of programs that are outside its constitutional mandate—from social welfare programs, education, public power, agriculture, public housing, urban renewal and all the other activities that can be better performed by lower levels of government or by private institutions or by individuals."[36]

This was not laissez-faire or libertarian philosophy, but an application of the Catholic principle of subsidiarity—a principle that candidate Ronald Reagan had promised he would follow if elected president (as with, for example, his promise to abolish the Department of Education). But Reagan was generally unsuccessful in rolling back the welfare state, undone by opposition in his administration as well as Congress. Subsequent presidents had had no more luck. Indeed, as Buckley noted in his November 2007 interview, conservatives had allowed the state to grow too large and powerful, forgetting the warnings of Albert Jay Nock and others.

Anthony Dick, the Stanford law student who served as research assistant on the Goldwater memoir, said that the eighty-one-year-old Buckley kept an exhausting pace in writing the book. "I would go to bed tired each night and come down for breakfast at eight each morning, and he would already be up in the study, attacking the next chapter, Bach on the stereo, sailboats bobbing in the water down below." (They worked in a rented house in Bermuda.)

When the young man remarked how nice it must be, doing the things he loved, Buckley quickly corrected him. He found writing increasingly difficult. Nor did he love politics, which he said was awash in sordidness and banality. He would much prefer to read or sail or visit friends, but he stayed at work—echoing what he had told Peter Robinson and others—out of a sense of duty to his country, to repay civilization for all the beauty it had given him, and to resist the designs of those "who would push the tentacles of politics even farther into our lives."[37]

Flying High was the penultimate book. In between squirts of oxygen and notes to old friends, Buckley spent six weeks at the end of 2007 and into the first month of 2008 completing his Reagan memoir—with the help of Danilo Petranovich, the last in a long line of young research assistants stretching back more than forty years.

The Reagan I Knew includes private letters, recorded exchanges, and personal reminiscences on such matters as the INF treaty (Reagan kept reassuring Buckley), Supreme Court nominees (Buckley urged the nomination of Robert Bork), the Reagan children (both Ron Jr. and Patti frequently wrote to Buckley—Ron Jr. addressing him as "Uncle Bill"), and Buckley's secret mission as "ambassador" to Afghanistan.

Missing from the memoir is Reagan's warm "Happy Birthday" letter to Buckley, dated November 24, 1994, less than three weeks after the former president had announced to "my fellow Americans" that he had Alzheimer's. Reagan wrote Buckley: "As I get on in years and reflect back on those individuals who have meant the most to me throughout my lifetime, I am grateful for you and the many ways in which you have touched my life. Nancy and I are blessed to know you and call you a friend."[38]

Buckley and Reagan genuinely enjoyed each other's company; not even their sharp differences over the disposition of the Panama Canal treaties—which Reagan opposed and Buckley supported—could affect the friendship. Three months after their nationally televised debate about the treaties in January 1978, Buckley was invited to the Reagan home in Pacific Palisades for dinner. "Drive carefully as you approach the house," Reagan instructed his guest. "I have special instructions for you on my driveway." Buckley did as he was told.

At intervals of twenty yards along the driveway were hand-painted cardboard signs that read, in sequence:

WE BUILT IT

WE PAID FOR IT

IT'S OURS![39]

Although the Senate ratified the Panama Canal treaties, Buckley believed—as did other conservatives—that Reagan's conspicuous opposition combined with President Carter's enthusiastic embrace of the treaties helped make possible his election as president in 1980.

It may be that as Buckley worked on the Reagan memoir he was considering his next book—perhaps a look at the early tumultuous days of *National Review,* when he was surrounded by some of the most brilliant and opinionated writers in America and persuaded them to fight the socialists and the Communists, not one another. But on February 27, 2008, death came for the most eloquent conservative of the twentieth century. There would be no more words from the master of words.

CODA

He was *the* maker of the American conservative movement—a master fusionist.

Until Bill Buckley came along, says William A. Rusher, who worked beside him for thirty years as publisher of *National Review,* "there was a congeries of ill assorted half-enemies. He brought them together into a unified movement by pointing out they all had the same enemy—the liberals."[1]

"He did it all," says *NR* editor Rich Lowry. "He combined George Will, the columnist; Rush Limbaugh, the voice; Tim Russert, the interviewer; Ann Coulter, the liberals' bête noir; and Tom Clancy, the novelist."[2]

Because of his life and work, says National Review Online editor Kathryn Lopez, "conservatives will never be seriously lost in the wilderness."[3]

He was philosophically conservative but temperamentally free-spirited. He was fearless, says Thomas (Dusty)

Rhodes, chairman of *National Review.* "Nothing got to him, sailing, skiing, nothing." His courage derived from his religion—he believed "he was going to Heaven." Frances Bronson, his personal assistant for four decades, agrees: "His faith was his grounding."[4]

He never pandered in his writing. Says *NR* senior editor Jay Nordlinger, he sought "the right word, not just big words."[5]

He could not bear to be idle or without a book. "His nightmare," says Kate O'Beirne, president of the National Review Institute, "was to be stuck somewhere where he had nothing to read—not even at a street corner."[6]

Among the books that made a difference in his life— Albert Jay Nock's *Memoirs of a Superfluous Man* and Bruce Marshall's *Father Malachy's Miracle.*

He revered his father, he loved Our Lady, and he was bereft when his wife, Pat, died before he did.

He viewed Communism as the great enemy of America and the West, an enemy to be defeated, not accommodated.

He saw his goals achieved, says longtime friend and colleague Daniel Oliver: "Communism defeated, free market economics widely understood if not widely enough practiced, and some sense that government could be, not the solution, but the problem."[7]

He will live on in the sturdy journal of conservative opinion he founded; in his books, columns, speeches, and debates; in television interviews by him and of him; in the editorials, reviews, forewords, and letters he composed; in a mighty stream of words unequalled—according to the historian George Nash—by any writer of the last century.

Bill Buckley could have been the playboy of the Western world but chose instead to be the St. Paul of the modern American conservative movement. His vision of ordered liberty shaped and molded and guided American conservatism from its infancy to its maturity, from a cramped suite of offices on Manhattan's East Side to the Oval Office of the White House, from a set of "irritable mental gestures" to a political force that transformed American politics.

Notes

Preface

1. George Weigel, "Remembering Bill Buckley," posted on "The Catholic Difference" at eppc.org, April 9, 2008.

2. Reverend George W. Rutler, "Bethany Was Near Jerusalem," homily at the Memorial of William F. Buckley Jr., St. Patrick's Cathedral, New York City, April 4, 2008.

3. A contribution by Nicholas Lemann to a retrospective in the *Wall Street Journal* entitled "Before Goldwater or Reagan, There Was Buckley," February 27, 2008.

4. Christopher Buckley, "A Eulogy for My Father," St. Patrick's Cathedral, April 4, 2008.

5. Ibid.

6. Ibid.

7. Michael Barone, "Buckley: A History Changer," *U.S. News & World Report*, February 28, 2008.

8. Henry A. Kissinger, "Last Voyage," St. Patrick's Cathedral, April 4, 2008.

9. Ibid.

10. Rush Limbaugh, "Buckley Was My Greatest Inspiration," Newsmax. com, February 27, 2008; also, "Rush Accepts Media Research Center's 'William F. Buckley Jr. Award for Media Excellence,'" RushLimbaugh. com, March 30, 2007.

11. William Kristol, "The Indispensable Man," *New York Times*, March 3, 2008.

12. Michael Kinsley, "Kinsley on Intellectual Honesty," *Slate*, February 28, 2008.

13. "William F. Buckley Jr., Champion of Conservatism, Dies at 82," *International Herald Tribune*, February 27, 2008.

14. Christopher Hitchens, "A Man of Incessant Labor," *Weekly Standard*, March 10, 2008.

15. Tim Russert, "A Singular Force in American Life," from a lecture at Notre Dame University, April 14, 2008, quoted at phibetacons.nationalreview.com.

16. Christopher Westley, "William Buckley's Permanent Thing," LewRockwell.com, February 28, 2008; Lew Rockwell, "William F. Buckley, Jr., RIP," LewRockwell.com/blog, February 27, 2008.

17. Paul Gottfried, "Marvels and Missed Opportunities," takimag.com, March 5, 2008.

18. "William F. Buckley Jr., Champion of Conservatism, Dies at 82," *International Herald Tribune*.

CHAPTER 1

1. Linda Bridges and John R. Coyne Jr., *Strictly Right: William F. Buckley Jr. and the American Conservative Movement* (Hoboken, NJ: John Wiley & Sons, 2007), 10.

2. John B. Judis, *William F. Buckley Jr.: Patron Saint of the Conservatives* (New York: Simon and Schuster, 1988), 31.

3. Ibid., 31–32.

4. William F. Buckley Jr., *Miles Gone By: A Literary Autobiography* (Washington, DC: Regnery Publishing, 2004), 6.

5. Bridges and Coyne, 10.

6. Ibid., 12.

7. Judis, 40.

8. Buckley, *Miles Gone By,* 28, 35.

9. Judis, 36; William F. Buckley Jr., *Nearer, My God: An Autobiography of Faith* (New York: Doubleday, 1997), xx.

10. Priscilla L. Buckley and William F. Buckley Jr., eds., *W. F. B.—An Appreciation by His Family and Friends* (New York: Privately Printed, 1950), 243.

11. Ibid., 244.

12. Lee Edwards, *Reading the Right Books: A Guide for the Intelligent Conservative* (Washington, DC: The Heritage Foundation, 2007), 14.

13. Ibid.

14. WFB Jr. to Henry Regnery, July 8, 1963, Henry Regnery Papers, Hoover Institution, Stanford University, California.

15. Bridges and Coyne, 13.

16. Judis, 48.

17. Ibid., 50.

18. Ibid., 51.

19. Ibid., 54.

20. "Mr. Truman's Complex," editorial, *Yale Daily News,* May 14, 1949.

21. "For the Republican Conclave," *Yale Daily News,* April 30, 1949.

22. Judis, 71.

23. "A Call for an Indigenous Communist Party," *Yale Daily News,* March 23, 1948.

24. "An Easy Out," *Yale Daily News,* November 21, 1949.

25. "The Problems at Hand," *Yale Daily News,* September 24, 1949; "Needed: A Little Intolerance." *Yale Daily News,* October 12, 1949; editor's note, *Yale Daily News,* December 12, 1949.

26. Judis, 67.

27. Ibid.

28. Ibid, 68.

29. Ibid.

30. Ibid., 75.

31. "Exit," *Yale Daily News,* January 20, 1950.

32. Judis, 66.

33. Buckley, *Miles Gone By,* 105.

34. Bridges and Coyne, 16.

35. Judis, 57.

36. Bridges and Coyne, 16.

37. George H. Nash, *The Conservative Intellectual Movement in America Since 1945* (Wilmington, DE: Intercollegiate Studies Institute, 1996), 212.

38. Ibid.

39. Ibid., 214.

40. George W. Carey, "Willmoore Kendall," *American Conservatism: An Encyclopedia* (Wilmington, DE: ISI Books, 2006), 464.

41. Ibid., 465.

42. Ibid.

43. Judis, 61–62.

44. WFB Jr. to Henry Regnery, September 1950, Regnery Papers, Hoover Institution.

45. Carey, 465.

46. Nash, 217.

47. Buckley, *Miles Gone By,* 58.

48. Judis, 64.

49. John Bartlett, *Familiar Quotations* (Boston: Little, Brown and Company, 1938), 25.

50. Bridges and Coyne, 18.

51. Ibid.

52. Ibid.

53. Judis, 69.

54. William F. Buckley Jr., "Patricia Taylor Buckley, R. I. P.," *National Review,* May 14, 2007.

55. Ibid, 80.

56. Arthur Koestler in Andre Gide, Richard Wright, Ignazio Silone, Stephen Spender, Arthur Koestler, and Louis Fischer, *The God That Failed* (New York: Bantam Books, 1959), 54.

57. WFB to James Burnham, undated circa 1970, James Burnham Papers, Hoover Institution, Stanford University, California.

58. Ibid.

59. Henry Regnery to WFB Jr., October 26, 1951, Regnery Papers, Hoover Institution.

60. Buckley, *Miles Gone By,* 74.

61. Bridges and Coyne, 23.

62. William F. Buckley Jr., *God and Man at Yale: The Superstitions of "Academic Freedom"* (Chicago: Henry Regnery Company, 1951), 113.

63. Judis, 86.

64. William F. Buckley Jr., "Harvard Hogs the Headlines," *Human Events,* May 16, 1951.

65. William F. Buckley Jr. to E. Victor Milione, June 6, 1960, Buckley Papers, Sterling Library, Yale University, New Haven, Connecticut.

66. Frank Chodorov to WFB, December 5, 1951, Buckley Papers, Sterling Library, Yale.

67. Judis, 92.

68. Ibid., 98.

69. Lee Edwards, *Educating for Liberty: The First Half-Century of the Intercollegiate Studies Institute* (Washington, DC: Regnery Publishing, 2003), 11–12, 14.

70. Nash, 133.

71. Judis, 114.

72. Ibid., 112.

73. Ibid., 117.

74. Ibid.

75. Ibid., 118.

76. WFB Jr. to James Burnham, memorandum undated, circa 1957, James Burnham Papers, Hoover Institution.

77. Nash, 98–99.

78. Lee Edwards, *The Conservative Revolution: The Movement That Remade America* (New York: The Free Press, 1999), 36.

79. William F. Buckley Jr. and L. Brent Bozell, *McCarthy and His Enemies: The Record and Its Meaning* (Chicago: Henry Regnery Company, 1954), 335.

80. Judis, 110.

81. Ibid.

82. William F. Buckley Jr., "Tail Gunner Joe," *A Hymnal: The Controversial Arts* (New York: G. P. Putnam's Sons, 1978), 156.

83. Sam Tanenhaus, "W. F. Buckley's Auto-Revisionism," *Fortune,* June 7, 1999.

84. William F. Buckley Jr., "Tailgunner Ann," *Claremont Review of Books,* Winter 2003.

85. William F. Buckley Jr., "The Party and the Deep Blue Sea," *Commonweal,* January 25, 1952, 392–93.

CHAPTER 2

1. Nash, 142.
2. Robert H. W. Welch Jr. to Victor Lasky, October 26, 1955, Buckley Papers, Sterling Library, Yale. Lasky, a prominent anti-Communist author, wrote Welch asking for a statement supporting *National Review.*
3. J. Howard Pew to WFB, November 7, 1955, Buckley Papers, Sterling Library, Yale University.
4. Judis, 129.
5. Nash, 146.
6. WFB to Russell Kirk, September 14, 1955, Buckley Papers, Sterling Library, Yale.
7. Judis, 126.
8. Jeffrey Hart, *The Making of the American Conservative Mind:* National Review *and Its Times* (Wilmington, DE: ISI Books, 2005), 12–13.
9. Buckley, *Miles Gone By,* 317.
10. Whittaker Chambers, *Witness* (Washington, DC: Regnery Gateway, 1987), 11–12.
11. Nash, 134.
12. Ibid., 135.
13. William F. Buckley Jr., "Memorandum Re: A New Magazine," circa 1954, Regnery Papers, Hoover Institution.
14. Ibid.
15. Bridges and Coyne, 41.
16. Ibid.
17. *The* National Review *Reader,* edited by John Chamberlain (New York: The Bookmailer, 1975), 24; Judis, 141; Bridges and Coyne, 43.
18. Nash, 138.
19. Ibid., 140.
20. Ibid., 139.
21. Linda Bridges to the author via email, December 1, 2008.
22. Jeffrey Hart, "Dazzler," *National Review,* March 24, 2008, 34.

23. Jameson Campaigne Jr. to the author, March 23, 1998.

24. Nicole Hoplin and Ron Robinson, *Funding Fathers: The Unsung Heroes of the Conservative Movement* (Washington, DC: Regnery Publishing, 2008), 79.

25. Dom Damian Kearney, "Some Recollections of William F. Buckley at Yale and Portsmouth," *Portsmouth Abbey School Bulletin*, Summer 2008, 41.

26. William F. Buckley Jr., *Let Us Talk of Many Things: The Collected Speeches* (Roseville, CA: Forum, 2000), xxvii.

27. Zachary Cook, "Buckley Brings Wit to Conservatism, to Chapin," *Williams Record*, April 23, 1993.

28. Willliam F. Buckley Jr., *Up from Liberalism* (New York: McDowell, Obolensky, 1959), 5, 197.

29. Ibid., 202–3.

30. Bridges and Coyne, 45.

31. Ibid., 46.

32. Ibid., 47.

33. Frank S. Meyer to William F. Buckley Jr., and other senior *NR* editors, May 10, 1960, Buckley Papers, Sterling Library, Yale University.

34. James Burnham to William F. Buckley Jr., October 9, 1960, Buckley Papers, Sterling Library, Yale University.

35. "*National Review* and the 1960 Elections," *National Review,* October 22, 1960, 234.

36. Judis, 175.

37. For an extended discussion of the Sharon Conference, see John A. Andrew III, *The Other Side of the Sixties: Young Americans for Freedom and the Rise of Conservative Politics* (New Brunswick, NJ: Rutgers University Press, 1997), 53–74.

38. Ibid., 190.

39. Memorandum of William F. Buckley Jr., January 21, 1957, Buckley Papers, Sterling Library, Yale University.

40. Ibid.

41. William F. Buckley Jr., "Ayn Rand, R. I. P.," *Right Reason* (Garden City, NY: Doubleday & Company, 1985), 410.

42. Whittaker Chambers, "Big Sister Is Watching You," *National Review,* December 28, 1957, 594–596.

43. Nash, 144–45.

44. William F. Buckley Jr., "Notes Toward an Empirical Definition of Conservatism," in William F. Buckley Jr., *The Jeweler's Eye: A Book of Irresistible Political Reflections* (New York: G. P. Putnam's Sons, 1968), 18–19, 21–22.

45. Ibid.

46. Ibid., 27, 30.

47. William A. Rusher, *The Rise of the Right* (New York: Morrow, 1984), 117.

48. "John Birch Society," *American Conservatism: An Encyclopedia,* edited by Bruce Frohnen, Jeremy Beer, and Jeffrey O. Nelson (Wil-mington, DE: ISI Books, 2006), 456; William F. Buckley Jr., "Goldwater, the John Birch Society, and Me," *Commentary,* March 2008.

49. "The Question of Robert Welch," *National Review,* February 13, 1962, 83–88.

50. Bridges and Coyne, 75.

51. Judis, 173.

52. Hart, 321; Nash, 338.

53. Introduction by John O'Sullivan in William F. Buckley Jr., *In Search of Anti-Semitism* (New York: Continuum, 1992), xi–xii.

54. Bridges and Coyne, 271, 324. .

55. Joseph Sobran, "How I Was Fired by Bill Buckley," mecfilms.com/ universe c 1994; "The Real Bill Buckley," Griffin Internet Syndicate, May 30, 2006.

56. Jonathan Tobin, "Bill Buckley and the Jews," *Jewish World Review,* March 3, 2008.

57. Patrick Allitt, *The Conservatives: Ideas and Personalities Throughout American History* (New Haven, CT: Yale University Press, 2009), 194.

58. Bridges and Coyne, 81.

59. Edwards, *The Conservative Revolution,* 107.

60. See L. Brent Bozell, "Freedom or Virtue?" *National Review,* September 11, 1962, 181.

61. John Adams, letter to Mercy Warren, April 16, 1776, as quoted in *The Founders' Almanac,* ed. Matthew Spalding (Washington, DC: The Heritage Foundation, 2002), 207–8.

62. Edwards, *The Conservative Revolution,* 108.

63. Nash, 161.

64. William F. Buckley Jr., "Notes Toward an Empirical Definition of Conservatism," *What Is Conservatism?* edited by Frank S. Meyer (New York: Holt, Rinehart and Winston, 1964), 226.

65. William F. Buckley Jr., "Who Won? They Did," November 4, 1962.

66. Bridges and Coyne, 74.

67. Judis, 208.

68. Ibid., 209.

69. William F. Buckley Jr., *Rumbles Left and Right: A Book About Troublesome People and Ideas* (New York: G. P. Putnam's Sons, 1963), 68

70. Ibid., 59.

71. Ibid., 86.

72. Judis, 179.

CHAPTER 3

1. As recounted by Buckley biographer Linda Bridges to the author, December 15, 2008.

2. WFB interview with the author, November 15, 1994, New York City.

3. Bridges and Coyne, 79.

4. Ibid., 80.

5. Judis, 218.

6. "The Sniper," *Time*, November 3, 1967, 71.

7. Bridges and Coyne, 83.

8. Nash, 273.

9. See Judis, 228, regarding Buckley's intention to ask Goldwater to withdraw if he lost the California primary; and Lee Edwards, *Goldwater: The Man Who Made a Revolution* (Washington, DC: Regnery Publishing, 1995), 228, for F. Clifton White's evaluation of the Goldwater delegates.

10. Judis, 228.

11. Ibid., 230–31.

12. Ibid., 232.

13. Ibid.

14. WFB to Barry Goldwater, November 4, 1964, Buckley Papers, Sterling Library, Yale University.

202 ⊳ NOTES

15. According to Henry Regnery in his letter to WFB, November 24, 1975, Regnery Papers, Hoover Archives, Stanford University, Palo Alto, California.

16. Judis, 234.

17. John O'Sullivan, "Man of Thought, Man of Action," *National Review,* March 24, 2008, 24.

18. Edwards, *The Conservative Revolution,* 146.

19. Ibid.

20. Ibid., 147.

21. Ibid.

22. Ibid., 148.

23. Ibid., 149.

24. Bridges and Coyne, 96.

25. "The Sniper," 70.

26. See WFB's summary of these "interviews" in William F. Buckley Jr., *On the Firing Line: The Public Life of Our Public Figures* (New York: Random House, 1989), xxxii.

27. Ibid., xxx.

28. Ibid., 448.

29. Ibid.

30. Ibid., 449–50.

31. Ibid., 464–65.

32. Judis, 259.

33. Hart, 171.

34. Judis, 268–70.

35. Hart, 176.

36. Bridges and Coyne, 111–12.

37. Judis, 293–94.

38. Hart, 181.

39. Judis, 279.

40. Bill Rusher Memo to WFB and other *NR* editors, October 26, 1965, Buckley Papers, Sterling Library, Yale University.

41. Ibid., 283–85.

42. Bridges and Coyne, 138.

43. Ibid., 143.

44. William F. Buckley Jr., *United Nations Journal: A Delegate's Odyssey* (New York: Anchor Books, 1977), xxv.

45. Ibid., 237.

46. Bridges and Coyne, 147.

47. Judis, 360.

48. WFB to Ronald Reagan, October 24, 1973; WFB to Reagan, July 29, 1974, Buckley Papers, Sterling Library, Yale University.

49. Ronald Reagan to WFB, February 6, 1974, Buckley Papers, Sterling Library, Yale University.

50. Edwards, *The Conservative Revolution,* 179.

51. Ibid.

52. Ibid., 183.

53. Ibid., 188.

54. Judis, 369.

55. Ibid., 379.

56. Ibid.

57. Richard A. Viguerie, *The New Right: We're Ready to Lead* (Falls Church, VA: The Viguerie Company, 1980), 41–42.

58. Edwards, *The Conservative Revolution,* 193.

59. Judis, 326–27.

60. William F. Buckley Jr., *Four Reforms: A Guide for the Seventies* (New York: G. P. Putnam's Sons, 1973), 16, 31.

61. Daniel Patrick Moynihan, "Prescription from a Man Who Doesn't Trust Government," *New York Times Book Review,* January 13, 1974.

62. Ibid.

63. Buckley, *Four Reforms,* 85.

64. Ibid., 104.

65. Ibid., Inside Back Cover.

66. Linda Bridges, "The Irrepressible," *National Review,* March 24, 2008, 48.

67. Brian Domitrovic, "A Time for Action: William F. Buckley, *National Review,* and the Defeat of Stagflation," *Intercollegiate Review,* Fall 2008, 34–43; Buckley, *On the Firing Line,* 286.

68. Buckley, *Miles Gone By,* 344.

69. Ibid., 346–347.

70. Christopher Buckley, "My Old Man and the Sea," Portsmouth Abbey School, *Summer Bulletin 2008,* 42.

71. Ibid., 45.

72. Ibid.

CHAPTER 4

1. William F. Buckley Jr., *The Reagan I Knew* (New York: Basic Books, 2008), 5.

2. Ibid.

3. See the appendix of Thomas Paine, *Common Sense* (Rockville, MD: Arc Manor, 2008), 71.

4. Judis, 382.

5. William F. Buckley Jr., "Remarks (Excerpted) at the Anniversary Dinner," *National Review,* December 5, 1975.

6. Judis, 283–84.

7. Edwards, *The Conservative Revolution,* 189.

8. Alfred S. Regnery, *Upstream: The Ascendance of American Conservatism* (New York: Threshold Editions, 2008), 266–67.

9. Lee Edwards, *A Brief History of the Modern American Conservative Movement* (Washington, DC: The Heritage Foundation, 2004), 67.

10. Bridges and Coyne, 192.

11. Austin Ranney, *The American Elections of 1980* (Washington, DC: AEI Press, 1981), 31.

12. Bridges and Coyne, 207.

13. Ibid., 210.

14. Judis, 416–17.

15. Ibid., 421.

16. William F. Buckley Jr., "The Animating Indiscretions of Ronald Reagan," excerpted from *Let Us Talk of Many Things: The Collected Speeches* (Roseville, CA: Forum, 2000), 457–64.

17. Buckley, *Rumbles Left and Right,* 134.

18. "Start of a New Era," *U.S. News & World Report,* November 17, 1980, 21–66, 90–110; "That Winning Smile," *Time,* November 17, 1980, 20–24ff; "Election Special," *Newsweek,* November 17, 1980, 27–34ff.

19. Judis, 425.

20. Ibid., 431.

21. Ibid., 435.

22. Hart, 263–64.

23. Ibid., 272–73.

24. Ibid., 281.

25. Ibid., 282.

26. Geoffrey Smith, *Reagan and Thatcher* (New York: W. W. Norton, 1991), 146; Lou Cannon, *President Reagan: The Role of a Lifetime* (New York: Public Affairs, 2000), 739.

27. Buckley, "The Courage of Friedrich Hayek," *Let Us Talk of Many Things,* 233.

28. "Moral Distinctions and Modern Warfare," in ibid., 298.

29. Bridges and Coyne, 233.

30. Ibid., 235.

31. Judis, 432.

32. Bridges and Coyne, 236.

33. Judis, 445.

34. Ibid., 452.

35. Bridges and Coyne, 248.

36. Lee Edwards, *The Essential Ronald Reagan: A Profile in Courage, Justice, and Wisdom* (Lanham, MD: Rowman & Littlefield, 2005), 123.

37. William F. Buckley Jr., "Nice Try," Universal Press Syndicate, September 15, 1987.

38. Lee Edwards, *To Preserve and Protect: The Life of Edwin Meese III* (Washington, DC: The Heritage Foundation, 2005), 86.

39. William F. Buckley Jr., "Understanding Meese," Universal Press Syndicate, October 28, 1986.

40. Buckley, *The Reagan I Knew,* 205–6.

41. Ibid.

42. Ibid., 209.

43. WFB notes of a telephone conversation between President Ronald Reagan and Buckley, September 1987, Buckley-Reagan Correspondence, Offices of National Review.

44. Bridges and Coyne, 257–58.

45. Edwards, *The Essential Ronald Reagan,* 147.

46. As confirmed in an email from Mal Kline to the author, January 4, 2010. Kline is an unofficial Boswell to Evans, who has used the cesspool/ hot-tub analogy for years.

47. For a detailed examination of the breakup, see Richard Brookhiser, *Right Time, Right Place: Coming of Age with William F. Buckley Jr. and the Conservative Movement* (New York: Basic Books, 2009).

48. Buckley, "Time to Go to Bed," *Let Us Talk of Many Things*, 362.

49. Bridges and Coyne, 272.

50. Ibid, 278.

51. O'Sullivan, "Man of Thought, Man of Action," 26.

52. Buckley, "The Greatness of James Burnham," *Let Us Talk of Many Things*, 271.

53. William F. Buckley Jr., "Russell Kirk, RIP," *National Review*, May 30, 1994.

54. William F. Buckley Jr, "Standing Athwart," *National Review*, December 11, 1995.

55. Ibid.

56. Bridges and Coyne, 299–300.

57. Interview with Rich Lowry, November 19, 2008, Washington, DC.

58. Rich Lowry, "A Personal Retrospective: *NR* and Its Founder," National Review Online, November 17, 2005.

59. Rich Lowry, *Legacy: Paying the Price for the Clinton Years* (Washington, DC: Regnery Publishing, 2003), 164.

60. Bridges and Coyne, 300.

61. William J. Bennett quote, inside flap, and Charles W. Colson quote, back cover, Buckley, *Nearer, My God*.

62. Ibid., 159–60.

63. Ibid., 276.

64. William F. Buckley Jr., "Barry Goldwater, RIP," *National Review*, June 22, 1998.

65. Barry Goldwater to WFB, February 24, 1983; WFB to Goldwater, March 17, 1983, Buckley Papers, Sterling Library, Yale University.

66. Buckley, "Preserving the Heritage," *Let Us Talk of Many Things*, 465–66.

67. Buckley, "The Genesis of Blackford Oakes," *Let Us Talk of Many Things*, 315.

68. William F. Buckley Jr., "Ronald Reagan: 1911–2004," *National Review*, June 28, 2004.

69. Buckley, *The Reagan I Knew*, 241.

70. Bridges and Coyne, 3.

CHAPTER 5

1. Buckley first used the formulation publicly in late 2005 in a *Wall Street Journal* interview but had privately used it before. Email from Linda Bridges to the author, January 4, 2010.

2. William F. Buckley Jr., "War on Hussein," Universal Press Syndicate, September 14, 2001.

3. William F. Buckley Jr., "Killing Bin Laden Won't Do," Universal Press Syndicate, October 5, 2001.

4. William F. Buckley Jr., "Evidence Against Iraq?" Universal Press Syndicate, October 9, 2001.

5. Rich Lowry, "A New Middle East," National Review Online, June 25, 2002.

6. William F. Buckley Jr., "Bush at the UN: Thoughts Said and UN Said," Universal Press Syndicate, October 13, 2002.

7. Buckley, "War on Hussein."

8. William F. Buckley Jr., "Great Words from W," Universal Press Syndicate, October 2, 2003.

9. David Frum, "Unpatriotic Conservatives: A War Against America," *National Review,* April 7, 2003, 40; David Keene, "Big Tent Needed for Conservatives of Every Stripe," *Hill,* June 3, 2003.

10. Owen Harries, "What Conservative Means," *American Conservative,* November 17, 2003.

11. William F. Buckley Jr., "'Lessons to Take,'" Universal Press Syndicate, July 2, 2004.

12. Editorial, "An End to Illusion," *National Review,* April 16, 2004.

13. William F. Buckley Jr., "Should We Have Gone to War?" Universal Press Syndicate, July 13, 2004; David D. Kirkpatrick, "*National Review* Founder Says It's Time to Leave Stage," *New York Times,* June 29, 2004.

14. Buckley, "Should We Have Gone to War?"

15. Lew Rockwell, "The Great Conservative Hoax," May 8, 2006 (as reprinted in the Huffington Post, December 30, 2009).

16. For the Buckley-Podhoretz exchange, see Josh Marshall, talkingpointsmemo.com, June 25, 2007.

17. Editorial, "The Day That Binds," *National Review,* June 29, 2005.

18. "George Will and William F. Buckley," *This Week,* ABC News, October 9, 2005.

19. Joseph Rago, "Old School: William F. Buckley Explains Why He Thinks Conservatism Has Become 'a Little Bit Slothful,'" *Wall Street Journal,* November 12, 2005.

20. Ibid.

21. Jeffrey Hart, "Right at the End: William F. Buckley's Last Gift to Conservatism May Have Been His Opposition to the Iraq War," *American Conservative,* March 24, 2008.

22. WFB's statement to Evan Galbraith is from the author's interview with Rich Lowry, November 19, 2008. For the quotation about the surge, see William F. Buckley Jr., "Yes or No to Bush?" National Review Online, January 15, 2007.

23. Rich Lowry, "The End of Illusion, Part II," King Features Syndicate, September 19, 2008.

24. Bridges and Coyne, 323.

25. William F. Buckley Jr., *Gratitude: Reflections on What We Owe to Our Country* (New York: Random House, 1990), 155.

26. William F. Buckley, Jr., "Patricia Taylor Buckley, R. I. P.," *National Review,* May 14, 2007.

27. William F. Buckley Jr., "My Smoking Confessional," Universal Press Syndicate, December 3, 2007.

28. William F. Buckley Jr., remarks at the awards banquet of the Victims of Communism Memorial Foundation, Washington, DC, June 12, 2007.

29. Lee Edwards, "Catholic Maverick," *Crisis,* February 1995, 40–41.

30. Interview with Rich Lowry, November 19, 2008.

31. Terry Eastland, "The Gift of Friendship," *Weekly Standard,* March 10, 2008.

32. Bill Steigerwald, "William F. Buckley—A Nov. 14, 2007 Interview," Townhall.com.

33. William F. Buckley Jr., "Fowlerspeak—Goodspeak," Universal Press Syndicate, February 1, 2008.

34. George Orwell, "Politics and the English Language," *Horizon,* April 1946.

35. Lee Edwards, "Principled and Pilloried," *Wall Street Journal,* May 2, 2008.

36. William F. Buckley Jr., *Flying High: Remembering Barry Goldwater* (New York: Basic Books, 2008), 121.

37. Anthony Dick, "Apolitico," *National Review,* March 24, 2008, 60.

38. Ronald Reagan to WFB, November 24, 1994, Buckley-Reagan Correspondence, Offices of National Review, New York City.

39. Buckley, *The Reagan I Knew,* 111.

CODA

1. Interview with William A. Rusher, September 11, 2008.

2. Interview with Rich Lowry, November 19, 2008.

3. Kathryn Jean Lopez, "Gratitude," National Review Online, November 26, 2008.

4. Interviews with Thomas L. (Dusty) Rhodes, November 6, 2008, and Frances Bronson, November 6, 2008.

5. Interview with Jay Nordlinger, November 6, 2008.

6. Interview with Kate O'Beirne, October 27, 2008.

7. Daniel Oliver, "Bill Buckley: A Life 'On the Right,'" from remarks delivered at the Heritage Foundation's thirty-first annual Resource Bank, Atlanta, Georgia, April 24, 2008, and reprinted in the Summer 2008 issue of *Insider,* a Heritage publication.

ACKNOWLEDGMENTS

I begin by acknowledging that Bill Buckley published my first article in *National Review* and that he encouraged my varied conservative and anti-Communist enterprises, often traveling hundreds of miles to give a speech at an event or narrate a film or simply lend his presence. I had long wanted to write a short intellectual biography of him, leaving to others the awesome challenge of sifting through the hundreds of boxes at Yale's Sterling Library and producing the "definitive" biography of the most influential conservative intellectual in America. I rest content with this work, made possible by the help of the ever available William R. Massa Jr., Yale University Library archivist; Linda Bridges, sterling editor, author, and WFB collaborator; the discerning insights of William A. Rusher, Rich Lowry, Jay Nordlinger, Kate O'Beirne, Frances Bronson, and other *NR* stalwarts; and research assistants Nicola Karras, Katherine Koerber, Benjamin Cole, Jaron Janson, Carol Browning Cooper, and Kevin Brooks. I remain indebted to Edwin J. Feulner, president of The Heritage Foundation, for his steady encouragement and Heritage's generous support of my research and writing. Jed Donahue of ISI Books is all that a writer can ask for in an editor, and I am also grateful to Bill Kauffman for his thoughtful edits. This is a much better book because of their suggestions and questions. The rest of the staff at ISI Books was equally helpful, especially Jennifer Fox, Chris Michalski, Christian Tappe, and ISI's president, T. Kenneth Cribb Jr. I conclude by acknowledging once again the irreplaceable help of the irreplaceable person in my life—my wife, Anne.

Lee Edwards
January 2010

Index